The Complete Guide to

Budgie Care and Ownership

Robert Mitchell

Publication Data

Robert Mitchell
The Complete Guide to Budgie Care and Ownership – First edition.
Summary: "Successfully caring for and owning a Budgie"
Provided by publisher.
ISBN: 978-1-961846-09-8
[1. The Complete Guide to Budgie Care and Ownership – Non-Fiction] I. Title.

This book has been written with the published intent to provide accurate and authoritative information in regard to the subject matter included. While every reasonable precaution has been taken in preparation of this book the author and publisher expressly disclaim responsibility for any errors, omissions, or adverse effects arising from the use or application of the information contained inside. The techniques and suggestions are to be used at the reader's discretion and are not to be considered a substitute for professional veterinary care. If you suspect a medical problem with your Budgie, consult your veterinarian.

Design by Sorin Rădulescu
First paperback edition, 2024

TABLE OF CONTENTS

Chapter 9

INTRODUCTION

Birds have always fascinated and entertained me, and none more so than the cheerful little budgie. Our first family pet was a budgie my parents received as a gift from an older couple who raised budgies in their small aviary in Southern California. I was not yet two when we acquired our feathered companion, and I have only a vague memory of this first of many budgies I would come to know over the years, but he must have made quite an impression on me at the time. My mother once confided, with a tinge of disappointment, that my first words were, "Hi bird."

What is it about budgies that makes them so appealing to children and adults the world over? Many people are surprised at how much personality these birds have. Budgies are highly social creatures, and are basically hard-wired to interact with other members of their flock, including their human caregivers. Because they are small, budgies are relatively

inexpensive to purchase, easy to care for, and they don't require as much space as larger pets. Budgies are also extremely intelligent. They can be trained to play games, perform a variety of tricks, perch on your shoulder, and even mimic human speech.

Budgies enrich the lives of their owners in many different ways, but the benefits of pet ownership also come with some responsibilities. Like other pets, budgies require an appropriate diet, physical exercise, mental stimulation, and a comfortable environment to stay happy and healthy. This book was written to give readers a good starting point for all aspects of budgie care, including purchasing the right bird, setting up the cage, feeding and handling, keeping your bird healthy, and breeding budgies. Whether you want to know more about budgies before you bring one into your home, or you already have a budgie and would like to know how to give your bird the best life possible, this book is designed to provide you with the essential information and expert guidance you need.

CHAPTER 1

What Is a Budgie?

Australia to England to America

Budgie Origin and History

The budgerigar, or budgie for short, is one of the most popular pets in the world. These small members of the parrot family are affectionate and playful, easy to train, and make wonderful companions for children and adults alike. Today, it's hard to imagine the world without these lively little birds, but 200 years ago, they were virtually unknown outside their native Australia.

The English zoologist George Shaw recorded the first scientific description of the budgie. While examining a bird specimen at the Natural History Department of the British Museum, Shaw realized he was looking at a unique species, and he called the bird an "undulated parrakeet." In 1805, he published his description along with a color illustration in the periodical *The Naturalist's Miscellany*. Many years later, the renowned ornithologist John Gould gave the budgie its full binominal name, *Melopsittacus undulatus*, which means "song parrot with wavy lines." The common name budgerigar was borrowed from Australian Aboriginal languages and initially transcribed by Gould as "betcherrygah." Although many people refer to this clever little bird as a parakeet, the term *parakeet* applies to about 115 species of small, seed-eating parrots with long, tapering tails and slender bodies. To avoid confusion, this book uses budgerigar and the shorter form "budgie" to refer to these pint-sized Australian parrots.

It was also John Gould who first introduced the budgie to bird enthusiasts in Europe. In 1838, John and his wife Elizabeth sailed to Australia on

DID YOU KNOW?
Budgie Clubs and Associations

Budgerigars or budgies are one of the most popular pet birds in America, so it's no surprise that several clubs are dedicated to them. The Budgerigar Association of America (BAA) is a place for budgie enthusiasts to learn more about these popular birds and how to show them at exhibitions. In addition, the BAA website hosts a list of affiliated budgie clubs, upcoming shows, and helpful articles about these birds. For more information, visit www.budgerigarassociation.org. The American Budgerigar Society (ABS) is another club option for North American budgie enthusiasts. Members of the ABS receive a bimonthly bulletin and enjoy access to exclusive ABS products. For more information, visit www.abs1.org.

an expedition to study native birds and write a comprehensive book on the subject. Elizabeth, an accomplished artist, joined her husband as one of the book illustrators. The result of their collaboration was *The Birds of Australia*, which was published in seven volumes between 1840 and 1848. Among the many illustrations Elizabeth contributed was a beautiful color portrait of wild budgies feeding on grass seed. When the Goulds returned to London in 1840, they brought back a pair of budgies that had been raised by Elizabeth's younger brother, Charles Coxen. John Gould described the birds as "the most animated, cheerful little creatures you can possibly imagine." The birds were relatively easy to breed in captivity, and they soon became fashionable pets in the homes of the wealthy.

As budgies gained widespread popularity in England and throughout Europe, they were exported from Australia by the thousands to meet the

growing demand. Concern over the vast number of budgies being caught and shipped out of the country prompted the Australian government to ban their export in 1894. By that time, aviaries in Europe were already supplying the market with the delightful little birds, and breeders were producing budgies with color variations that were very different from the natural green and yellow plumage that helped conceal them from predators in the wild. Budgies began to arrive in America in the 1920s, and by the 1950s and 1960s, they had become such a common household pet they sometimes appeared in celebrity photographs alongside their famous owners. Budgies were seen perching in the homes of actors Clint Eastwood and Marilyn Monroe and in the White House as pets of President John F. Kennedy's children.

Wild Budgies in Australia

Much of our knowledge about budgies has come from breeders and bird enthusiasts who study them in captivity. But biologists observing wild budgies in their natural environment have provided us with fascinating insights into their life cycles and behavior.

The budgie's native habitat is central Australia, where they are usually found in grasslands, scrublands, and open woodlands. Because rainfall is often irregular in these arid and semi-arid landscapes, budgies are nomadic and roam over much of the continent in a continual search for food and water. When a water source dries up or when grass seed is depleted in one area, budgies travel in large flocks and cover great distances to follow the rainfall and search for ripening grasslands. Although budgies are true nomads, their movements are still affected by the seasons, and they are likely to fly north during the summer to chase the monsoons and fly south in the winter to pursue seasonal rainstorms. A typical flock of budgies can range from a few birds to more than a hundred, but after a heavy rainfall, these wandering flocks sometimes merge into a massive swarm containing tens of thousands of birds, all whirling and turning in unison.

Wild budgies are slightly smaller than those bred in captivity, and on average, they are about seven inches long and weigh a little over one ounce. Their natural plumage is light green, with a yellow head and black scallop markings on their neck, back, and wings. This color combination helps camouflage them from predators, such as hawks and falcons when budgies are perching in trees or feeding on the ground. In the wild, budgies usually drink water in the early morning before they begin their search for food. They sometimes drink on the wing to avoid predators lurking near a waterhole, quickly gulping water and then flying off within a few seconds.

Budgies primarily eat seeds and grains from grasses and herbaceous plants, but they also eat a variety of fruits, berries, nuts, leaves, and small insects. To avoid filling their crops with indigestible material,

they use their specialized beak and tongue to remove the outer husk of a seed before swallowing the kernel. The upper beak is longer than the lower beak, and the budgie uses its flexible tongue to roll a seed between the two parts of the beak until the husk splits and comes off. Budgies are very gregarious creatures, and after eating and drinking, they seek out a shady place to rest in the middle of the day. During these social occasions, they often take the opportunity to groom each other, constantly chattering to reassure other flock members or raise an alarm when a predator is sighted.

Breeding can take place in any season, but wild budgies usually gather in colonies to breed when food and water are plentiful and conditions are more favorable for raising their young. When a flock locates a suitable nesting area, the birds begin mating and nest building. Wild Budgies often maintain the same mate through multiple breeding seasons. A male will try to impress a female by perching next to her and singing, and the two birds will preen each other. As the courtship progresses, the male will bob his head and offer the female regurgitated food to demonstrate his potential as a provider.

The hen bird chooses the nest site, usually a hollow cavity in a tree trunk, branch, or log lying on the ground. The hen will use her beak to shape the entrance of the nest into a round or oval hole about one and one-quarter to two and a half inches across, creating an opening just large enough for a budgie to squeeze through yet small enough to discourage predators from entering to eat the eggs or chicks. The hen might also cover the bottom of the nest with soft wood chips, leaves, or feathers. Despite the hen's best efforts to create a safe haven for her brood, eastern brown snakes and pythons sometimes work their way into nests that are lower to the ground and eat newborn chicks.

The hen lays four to eight white eggs on alternating days, and she takes full responsibility for incubating them. She sits on the clutch alone, relying on the cock bird to forage and bring her food. After about 18 days, the eggs begin to hatch at a rate of one egg every other day, so each of the chicks in the same nest is at a different stage of growth than the others.

Budgie chicks are blind and naked when they hatch, and for the first few days the hen feeds them a protein-rich secretion called crop-milk, which is full of antibodies and nutrients. The hen feeds the younger chicks first and then the older chicks. She instinctively provides each age group with the appropriate diet it needs.

Photo Courtesy of Diana Cook

The chicks open their eyes when they are 10 days old, and at this stage, they are covered in soft down. Meanwhile, the cock continues to search for food to support his growing family. When his crop is full, he returns to the nest to regurgitate food for his mate, who in turn feeds the chicks. After the chicks are about three weeks old, the cock will begin feeding them directly unless the hen insists on continuing to feed them by herself.

About 30 to 40 days after hatching, the young birds have grown wing and tail feathers and are now ready to fly. The parent birds call to their young and encourage them to leave the nest, and a new generation of budgies is soon ready to join the flock.

The Modern Popularity of Budgies

Soon after they first arrived in Europe in the 1840s, budgies captured the hearts of their owners. What makes these pocket-size parrots the most popular pet birds in the world? Budgies have a number of characteristics that people find appealing, including their compact size, colorful plumage, intelligence, cheerful personality, and their ability to mimic human speech.

Budgies are considered an excellent starter bird for people who love birds and are thinking about adopting one as a pet. Because they are small, budgies don't require a lot of space. A good cage and a few toys and accessories are all that is required to accommodate them, which makes budgies an excellent choice when larger pets are out of the question or when owners live in a smaller home or apartment. Budgies are also relatively inexpensive to purchase, and their primary diet consists of seeds and small servings of fresh greens and vegetables, so feeding them doesn't stretch the family budget.

Although the natural plumage of the ancestral wild budgie is predominantly green and yellow, breeders have produced birds in a seemingly endless variety of colors to delight their owners. Budgies raised in captivity are more commonly arrayed in a combination of green and yellow or blue and white feathers, but there are now around 30 recognized color combinations in hues that range from very bright to soft pastel.

Like other members of the parrot family, budgies are remarkably intelligent for their size. Researchers have found that budgies have a highly developed intellect and even display problem-solving skills. Similar to cats and dogs, budgies can recognize their owners, learn the names their owners give them, and can be trained to come when called. They can also be taught to perform tricks and play games. Budgies can learn to perch on your finger, climb a ladder, walk through a tunnel, fetch small items, and play with a small toy ball.

Budgies are affectionate, and they readily bond with their human owners. They are naturally curious and playful and make cheerful companions for all age groups. First-time budgie owners are often surprised at how much individual personality they display.

> **"**
>
> *Budgies make a great first-time pet. They're small, fairly quiet, and easy to take care of. Every budgie has its own personality, and they can also learn to talk. They can quickly become your best friend.*
>
> JENNIFER TAYLOR
> *Jennifer's Budgies, Ontario Canada*
>
> **"**

Budgies rank among the top five parrot species that can mimic human speech, sharing that distinction with African grey parrots, Amazon parrots, Eclectus parrots, and Indian ring-necked parrots. Not all budgies have such an impressive gift of gab, and male budgies are more inclined to talk than females, but just teaching a pet bird to say a few words or phrases can be great fun.

Budgie Anatomy

Body Shape and Size

Budgies are small, seed-eating parrots with long tail feathers and streamlined bodies. Although all budgies originated in Australia and belong to the same species, *Melopsittacus undulatus*, selective breeding in captivity has produced two basic types of pet birds that differ in color and body size from their wild cousins.

The American budgie that is available from most breeders and pet stores is slightly larger than a wild bird, averaging around seven to eight inches in length and weighing about one to 1.4 oz. American budgies are active birds, and with proper care, they will typically live between seven and 14 years in captivity.

In contrast, the English budgie is a much larger bird that was bred for shows and exhibitions. English budgies are around 10 to 12 inches long, and their average weight is between 1.6 and 2.2 ounces. These birds look more regal than their American counterparts, and they have larger, more rounded heads and fluffier feathers. English budgies are more docile birds, and their life span is comparatively shorter, ranging between five and seven years of age.

Knowing the basic parts of your budgie's anatomy can be very helpful when talking with other bird owners or consulting with a veterinarian.

Beak: The beak is made up of two parts, the upper and lower mandibles. The upper mandible is sharply pointed and longer than the lower mandible. The shape of the beak makes it an ideal tool for cracking and dehusking seeds.

Breast: The breast is the upper front part of the bird below the throat.

Cere: The cere is the fleshy band of tissue above the beak surrounding the nares. The color of the cere changes as a young bird develops, and it can be a good indicator of a bird's sex. Mature males usually have a dark blue cere, and mature females usually have a white, tan, or brown cere.

NOTE:

Males having a dark blue Cere color is accurate for birds who are primarily green or blue, but this is not the case for many mutations such as albino or lutino for example. In those birds, a male cere tends to be pink rather than blue.

Cheek Patch: The cheek patch is the triangular patch of blue, gray, silver, or violet feathers on the cheek, just below the eye. These feathers reflect ultraviolet light and play an important role during courtship.

Cloaca: The cloaca, or vent, is an opening just below the tail that serves as the combined outlet for the reproductive, intestinal, and urinary tracts of birds. When mating, birds momentarily press their cloacas together to transfer sperm from the male to the female.

Crop: The crop is a muscular internal pouch located at the top of the breast. It is part of a bird's digestive system and temporarily stores and predigests food before it enters the stomach. Budgies regurgitate food from their crop to feed their mate or developing chicks.

Crown: The top of the head is called the crown.

Ear Coverts: You can't see them, but budgies have small flat holes for ears that are located on each side of the head below the eyes. The ears are protected by delicate feathers called ear coverts.

Eyes: Budgies have much better eyesight than humans, and they can also see ultraviolet light. The eyes are located on either side of the head, providing them with a field of vision of about 300 degrees, which helps them detect predators.

Feet: The budgie's feet are zygodactyl, which means that two toes point forward and two toes point backward. This is the second most common toe arrangement among perching birds and provides more dexterity for grasping and moving from branch to branch in a tree.

Mantle: The triangular area of the back between the top of the wings.

Mask: The area of the budgie's face below the beak.

Nape: The nape is the back of the neck.

Nares: The nares are the bird's nostrils located at the top of the beak.

Primary Feathers: The long flight feathers on the outer edge of the wing and the farthest away from the body when the wing is extended

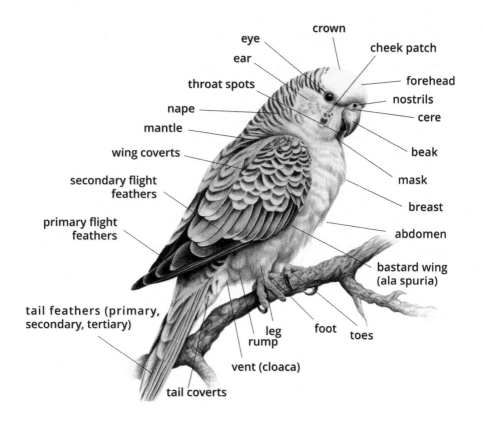

are the primary feathers. These feathers are responsible for propelling a bird forward and controlling direction. Budgies have 10 primary feathers on each wing.

Rump: The rump is the area above the tail on the lower back, and the uropygial gland is located here. This gland produces special oil that birds use to help waterproof their feathers and keep their beak supple. Budgies will rub their head and beak against this gland and then transfer the oil to their feathers and body.

Secondary Feathers: The shorter flight feathers on the inner edge of the wing and the closest to the body when the wing is extended are the secondary feathers. These feathers stay close together during flight to help sustain the bird in the air by giving it lift. Budgies have 11 secondary feathers on each wing.

Shoulder: The shoulder is the top of the wing next to the back.

Throat: The throat is the area below the beak, continuing down to the breast.

Throat Spots: These are the circular black spots along the base of the mask. Young budgies often have small, irregular spots, and mature birds have more distinct, rounded spots.

The Importance of Feathers and Colors

Feathers cover the bodies of all birds and enable them to fly. They also help birds stay warm and dry, camouflage them from predators, and play an important role in courtship displays. Meeting these various needs requires different types of feathers in an assortment of shapes and sizes. A healthy budgie will have around 2,000 to 3,000 feathers.

There are two basic types of feathers, all of which are made of keratin, the same protein that makes up a bird's skin, beak, and toenails. The larger feathers on the back, wings, and tail are called contour feathers. The more prominent contour feathers are the primary and secondary flight feathers on the wings and the primary, secondary, and tertiary tail feathers that help birds steer during flight and serve as a brake when the bird is landing. The smaller, fluffier feathers closest to the skin are called down feathers, and they primarily cover the chest and abdomen. The structure of the down feathers helps to trap air near the skin and insulate against heat loss.

Photo Courtesy of Alisha Morton

To keep their feathers in top condition, birds shed their worn and damaged feathers and replace them with new ones by molting. Adult budgies usually molt once a year, but some will molt once every six months. It is normal for your budgie to be missing some feathers during molting, but if you notice large bald spots, you should consult an avian veterinarian. Be sure to provide your budgie with a healthy, balanced diet during the molt so he will have all the necessary nutrients to grow beautiful new feathers.

Although budgies come in a wide array of colors, two basic components are responsible for much of this amazing variety. The first is pigment, and the second is the microscopic structure of the feathers themselves. Almost all budgies either have yellow pigment in their feathers and are classified as yellow-base birds, or they do not have this pigment and are classified as white-base birds. It is more common for yellow-base birds to have a combination of green and yellow feathers and for white-base birds to have a combination of blue and white feathers. Most budgies also have a structural blue color in their body feathers, which results from the way light reflects off the microscopic structure of the feathers. There is another component that affects the shade of color that is called the "dark factor." This is responsible for how light or how dark the various colors appear.

The subject of budgie color mutations can become quite complex, but what follows is a very simple explanation of how these pigment and structural components combine to produce such a wide variety of colors. If an artist blends yellow and blue paint together, the mixture will appear green. In a similar way, when a budgie has feathers that contain yellow pigment and a structural blue color, the feathers will appear green. Or, when feathers contain yellow pigment but lack a structural blue color, they will appear yellow. Likewise, when feathers lack yellow pigment but contain a structural blue color, the feathers will appear blue. This is how the variety of budgie color mutations arises from several basic components.

Speaking

Wild budgies constantly make a variety of sounds to communicate with other flock members or sound an alarm when danger appears. Your pet budgie will engage in similar "flock talk" to stay in contact with you and others that he considers part of the family, which might even include non-budgie pets. Budgies are not extremely loud, like some parrot species, and they are considered one of the quietest pet birds. Most people find their chirping and warbling a pleasant, cheerful addition to the home. But they are nevertheless very vocal, and if there is ambient noise or conversation in the room, they are likely to join in. They are wonderful mimics and will often imitate the common sounds they hear in their surrounding environment, including creaking doors, microwave ovens, and ringing cell phones. Some budgies have even learned to produce a convincing imitation of the whistles and beeps made by the robots in their owner's favorite sci-fi movie. Budgies can also be excellent talkers, but their interest and ability to talk varies from bird to bird. We'll discuss teaching your budgie to speak in Chapter 6.

FUN FACT

Talkative Bird

A budgie named Puck holds the Guinness World Record for the bird with the largest vocabulary. Puck lived in California with his owner, Camille Jordan, and learned to say 1,728 words before he died in 1994.

From Hatchling to Adult

Budgie eggs usually hatch after 18 to 23 days of incubation, and the eggs in the same clutch don't all hatch at the same time. They hatch one at a time about every other day in the order they were laid, so the first chick to hatch could be about 10 days old when the last of the chicks emerges from the shell.

It takes great effort for a baby budgie to peck its way out of the shell. About 24 hours before they hatch, budgie chicks begin to make chirping noises and start tapping on the shell from the inside to break free, using a sharp projection on their upper beak called an "egg tooth." The hen bird responds to these sounds by checking the eggs in the clutch more often. A chick will continue to peck around the end of the egg in a circle until it begins to open. With a final push of its tiny legs and wings, the hatchling emerges from the shell.

Blind and naked, budgie hatchlings look nothing like baby chickens or the adult birds they will become. Their eyes are closed, and their necks are too weak to hold up their heads. By the sixth or seventh day, their eyes open, and their primary feathers begin to appear. The hen feeds the chicks for the first 21 days. During this time, the cock provides support by regularly feeding the hen regurgitated food from his crop so that she doesn't have to leave the nest. After the first several weeks, the cock often assists the hen by feeding the chicks directly until they are fully weaned at about six weeks of age.

Budgies are ready to leave the nest when they are around four or five weeks old, but they will not reach full maturity until they are about eight months old. At four or five weeks, they are juvenile birds, and their appearance is noticeably different from adult birds until their first molt, which occurs when they are about three or four months old. The eyes of a juvenile bird are completely dark, without the lighter-colored irises around the pupils of adult birds. The feathers also help distinguish a juvenile from an adult bird. Juvenile budgies have stripes, or bars, all over the head and continuing down to the base of the upper beak. But after the first molt, the striped feathers on the cap—or top of the head—are replaced with solid white or yellow feathers.

Ask the Experts!

Do budgies make good pets for first-time bird owners?

Budgies are considered excellent pets for first-time bird owners due to their manageable size, relatively easy care, and engaging personalities. Experts highlight the minimal space required for their housing and their interactive nature when hand-raised. Budgies are known for their ability to learn tricks and talk, providing entertainment and companionship across various age groups. Their vibrant colors and potential for developing a strong bond with their owners add to the rewarding experience of owning a budgie.

" Budgies are one of the most underrated pet birds. If you get a sweet hand-fed or hand-tamed budgie, you can be guaranteed years of love, laughter, and nonstop entertainment. They are incredible first-time birds, but remember that no matter what type of bird you choose for your first pet, there will always be learning curves, frustrations, and challenges. Budgies, though small, have a huge personality and can be full of love and defiance. They can be balls of energy, but also the best little couch-potato friends. With the correct time and care, you will never be bored with your budgie. They are highly intelligent, bond very strongly to their people, and can learn to speak very well."

MISTY MARUSKA & MELODY MARUSKA,

Parrots N Stuff

" Budgies can definitely make good first-time pets if you take your time to research their behavior and the requirements for care! Budgies, though small, are extremely active and vocal little birds. It is good to be aware of the noise because while the noise level isn't extremely high, it can be pretty consistent. They are also not the cuddliest of species and tend not to settle in one spot for too long as they like to be moving! If you like an active and vocal pet, a budgie could be a great addition. Male budgies can also learn to speak very well if you put the time and effort into it."

SHANNON COCHRAN,

Chesapeake Aviary

❝ Budgies are great pets for first-time bird owners because they deliver a lot of 'bang for the buck.' Their housing takes up relatively little space. They are highly interactive with people when raised by hand. They often learn their own 'tricks' as well as talk. Budgies provide great entertainment and company for their owners, be they children, adults, or seniors."

SUSAN M. ANDRESEN,

Bull City Budgies

❝ Budgies make excellent pets for first-time bird owners because they are relatively easy-to-care-for birds, aren't expensive, are easy to tame, and have all the wonderful qualities we enjoy about birds. Budgies are easy to care for because, overall, they don't tend to be very picky about anything ... food, people, toys. It's rewarding to own them because they are very social birds who bond well with their humans. They are curious and smart, so introducing them to new foods and toys is easy."

LESLIE CORYN,

Featherbelle Aviary

CHAPTER 2

Is Budgie Life for You?

Social Creatures

Do you have the time to dedicate?

Although budgies are not as demanding as larger parrots, they are very active, social birds that need companionship to truly be happy. In nature, budgies live in flocks, and they instinctively bond with humans who regularly socialize with them. Before you decide to adopt a budgie, carefully

consider how much time you can afford to spend with your new friend. Can you give your budgie your undivided attention for at least one or two hours each day, in addition to the time you're simply working or relaxing in the same room as he chatters and plays? You don't have to focus attention on your budgie for a whole hour all at once; you can divide the time into a few short sessions throughout the day. Once you and your budgie have become friends, he will enjoy simply sitting on your shoulder while you read or watch TV. If you are willing to put in the time to develop a relationship with your budgie, he will soon accept you as a member of the flock.

It's also important to remember that your budgie will depend on you for all of his needs. Think carefully about the responsibility that entails as you consider whether a budgie will fit into your way of life. A healthy budgie can live for 10 to 15 years, which is less than some larger parrots but just as long as many dogs and cats. Cleaning the cage each week and daily feeding, watering, and playing with your pet are all part of the long-term commitment you make when you bring a budgie into your home. Think, too, about who will care for your budgie when you go on vacation or if an illness or injury requires that you spend some time in the hospital. Although they are small birds, budgies deserve just as much concern for their welfare as larger pets.

Training and handling

Some people enjoy training their budgies to perform a variety of tricks. Others just want their bird to act friendly and calm around humans. Whichever side of the training spectrum you start from, there are several basic skills that every budgie must learn that will encourage your bird to trust you and not become frightened when being handled or examined. These skills include teaching your budgie to step up onto your hand or finger, step onto a perch, and accept being gently held in a small towel. We will discuss how to train and safely handle your budgie in Chapter 6, but it's important to know that some basic training will be required to help your budgie become the wonderful companion that he has the potential to be.

One bird or two?

Should you adopt one budgie or two? In the wild, budgies spend their entire lives in large flocks. Budgies also tend to fare better in captivity when they are kept in pairs, and many budgie owners enjoy watching two or more

Photo Courtesy of Diana Cook

budgies interact with each other throughout the day, which can be very entertaining. On the other hand, single budgies are usually easier to train, more inclined to talk, and more likely to form a stronger bond with their owners. Which option is the right choice for you? Before deciding whether your budgie will be a solitary bird or have a companion, you will need to consider the advantages and disadvantages that each of these choices provides for you and your pet, and we will discuss them in detail in Chapter 3.

Ask the Experts!

One budgie or multiple?

Having multiple budgies can be beneficial because they provide companionship for each other, reducing loneliness and boredom. Budgies are naturally social and thrive in a flock environment, where they can engage in social behaviors, play, and communicate with each other. This can lead to happier and more active birds. However, it's important to balance this with the ability to tame and bond with individual birds, as multiple budgies may bond with each other more than with their human caregivers.

If you have more than one budgie, they will become a 'gang' and have lots of fun soaring around your home. However, if you want a bird that is devoted to people, especially if it has been hand-raised, stay with a single one. Multiple budgies will talk 'budgie' to each other and will likely lose the ability to speak 'human' if they gained it as a single bird."

SUSAN M. ANDRESEN,
Bull City budgies

Some benefits to owning multiple budgies are companionship for your budgies if you're not always home or around them all the time; you get to watch them interact with each other, play with each other, and there's more to love."

JENNIFER TAYLOR,
Jennifer's Budgies

" The majority of budgies will always do better with another bird of their own kind. We just cannot provide the amount of socialization that having another of the same species will provide. Budgies are gregarious flock animals. Some people believe they will not be able to bond with their budgies appropriately if they have more than one, but if you put in the effort and purchase from a breeder that has socialized their budgies to humans properly, then that should be of no concern."

SHANNON COCHRAN,
Chesapeake Aviary

" Multiple birds will eat better, molt better, and act more like birds. The interaction between two birds, whether male and female or two birds of the same gender, is so much more enjoyable to watch. However, it may make it more difficult to make good pets out of them, and their talking ability will be somewhat diminished."

PAUL LEWIS,
Birds Unlimited

" If you are wanting a pet bird/s for the noise and companionship but have no intentions of handling one on one, I would recommend getting two so that the birds have each other to bond to and entertain each other. Otherwise, if you want a relationship with your bird and to keep it nice, sweet, tame, and handleable, I would recommend just getting one. Once you add a second budgie and house them together, they will inevitably bond to each other over time and become more and more bird-oriented versus human-oriented. Their need for you to be their companion will likely go away, and eventually you will have two birds who love each other and want very little to nothing to do with you. People worry that with just one, the bird will be lonely while you are at work or away. This is where the proper supplies are essential. Having the proper toys for entertainment will allow the bird to self-entertain until you can get home and have one-on-one time with your bird."

MISTY MARUSKA & MELODY MARUSKA,
Parrots N Stuff

"Budgies are like potato chips ... The more colors you have, the more colors you see ... the more budgies you want. The fact is it depends on the type of relationship you want to have with your bird. If you want a bird to have a bond with you and be your best buddy, only get one. If you introduce multiple budgies together at the same time in the same cage, they will invariably bond with each other and you will be the third wheel. If you want to have budgies that are not tame but you enjoy watching them play in the cage together, you can get more than one and cage them together. If you want two budgies as pets, you should cage them separately but with the cages right next to each other, so they can see each other and talk to each other through the bars. Then you should focus on giving each budgie one-on-one time with you individually. This will establish your flock. You can then let them out to play together and with you. It all depends on what your desired relationship with your budgie will be."

LESLIE CORYN,
Featherbelle Aviary

Handle with Care

Fragile creatures

Like all birds, budgies are more fragile than most warm-blooded animals of similar size. Once they are used to their owners, budgies like to be handled and petted, but they must be treated gently. Here are a few things you should be aware of before adopting a budgie as a pet.

Loud noises and sudden movements can startle budgies and cause them to react wildly. When frightened, they often attempt to fly away from the perceived danger. If they do, they can injure themselves if they fly into a mirror or strike a window, lamp, or other piece of furniture.

Birds have a complex respiratory system that enables them to take in more oxygen during flight. When a budgie breathes, its ribs move in and out, so holding a budgie too tightly can restrict its breathing and may even cause death. The avian respiratory system includes special air sacs and hollow, air-filled bones that indirectly connect to the lungs. If one of these pneumatic bones is broken, the injury can make the lungs vulnerable to infection. And because their respiratory systems are so efficient, budgies are more sensitive than humans and many other pets to fumes from cigarette smoke, nonstick cookware, and household cleaners, so you should avoid exposing your bird to any of these and other potentially toxic fumes.

FUN FACT
The Smallest Parrot

Adult budgies generally reach a length of seven to eight inches, making them the second smallest parrot species in the world. The smallest parrot is the parrotlet, which typically grows four and a half to five inches long. Other small parrots include lovebirds, Bourke's parakeet, and Meyer's parrot.

Parrotlet

As a bird grows new feathers, the feathers emerge through the skin, and the shaft of the developing feather fills with blood. These immature feathers are called pinfeathers or blood feathers, and when damaged, they can bleed around the base. It is sometimes difficult to stop the bleeding when a pinfeather is injured, and a budgie can potentially lose a large amount of blood in a short time. If a damaged pinfeather continues to bleed, you should quickly contact your avian veterinarian for assistance.

Do you have other pets?

Safety is a primary concern when thinking about bringing a budgie into a household that already includes one or more pets. In general, prey animals such as rabbits, guinea pigs, and other small birds will often get along well with budgies that are kept in the same household. Many times, they just ignore each other, and sometimes interspecies friendships can develop. Even so, you should carefully monitor your pets when they are roaming the house outside their cages to make sure their interactions remain friendly. An otherwise friendly pet might be startled and react violently if a playful budgie were to land upon its head or nibble an ear.

Dogs and cats are naturally carnivorous, and many have a tendency to view a budgie as food rather than as part of the extended family. Cats are natural hunters, and they are often fascinated by birds. Birds can move very quickly, which may trigger a cat's hunting or play instincts and result in serious injury to a small bird. Even when you carefully monitor such interactions, you can never be fully in control of the situation.

In general, dogs are more likely to develop a peaceful relationship with a budgie. However, some dog breeds were intentionally developed for hunting small animals. No matter how friendly they are around humans, some dogs can never be trained not to chase and kill a small animal when the opportunity arises. Other dogs are more passive and inquisitive. For many years, a friend of mine had a black Labrador Retriever that formed a close bond with the family budgie, and he was always very gentle with the bird when it was out of its cage. The budgie clearly enjoyed the interaction with his canine friend and would call out the dog's name whenever he ambled into the room. But the size difference between dogs and budgies is so great that tragic accidents can happen if a dog misjudges things and plays too rough, so human supervision is always required when budgies are allowed to play outside their cage and another pet is in the room.

If your dog tends to be more amiable and you want to introduce him to your budgie, take things slowly. While keeping your dog under control, let her sniff the bird's cage and observe the bird. Calm the dog if she barks or jumps at the cage so that she understands that this behavior is not allowed. After a week or two, your dog will likely get used to having a bird in the house and will leave it alone.

If you have other pets, it doesn't necessarily mean that you cannot have a budgie. You can always keep budgies in a cage that is out of reach of larger pets and keep other pets out of the room when you let your budgie out of the cage to fly during exercise sessions.

Handling with children

Are there children in your home? Budgies make great pets for children who are old enough to understand how to handle them carefully and respectfully. Having a budgie in the home can also help parents teach

a child a sense of compassion and responsibility, which are valuable lessons that can last a lifetime.

Photo Courtesy of Alisha Morton

After your budgie has had some time to adjust to his new surroundings, he will enjoy being in the company of his new human family, including the children. But children need to learn how to properly interact with the new pet. Budgies can't be handled in the same way as a dog or a cat or held tightly like a doll. If children make loud noises or quick movements, they can frighten a small bird. So, it is important to explain to children that they should speak softly and avoid rapid gestures when they approach the budgie's cage or when they are allowed to handle the bird.

Will a child assist in caring for the new pet? Demonstrate how to properly refill the budgie's food and water dishes and how to change the cage lining every day. Don't take it for granted that children will automatically understand what they should or should not do when they interact with a budgie. After the budgie has received some basic training, be sure to teach your child how to handle it gently and safely. Explain that a budgie should never be taken outdoors or allowed to fly outside the cage without adult supervision. Consider making budgie playtime an activity that you and your child can share together. This will allow you to observe how your child behaves around the bird and will give you an opportunity to offer praise when a child acts appropriately or provide gentle correction when mistakes are made.

Ask the Experts!

Advice for New Owners

For new budgie owners, experts stress the importance of understanding budgie behavior, creating a stimulating environment, and ensuring proper nutrition. Familiarizing oneself with the bird's body language and vocalizations can improve communication and bond between owner and pet. Providing a variety of toys and changing them regularly can keep the budgie engaged and prevent boredom. Nutritionally, a balanced diet beyond just seeds, including fresh fruits and vegetables, is crucial for a budgie's health. Regular health checks and creating a safe living space are also emphasized to prevent accidents and detect health issues early.

> When you first bring home your new friend, give him time and space to get used to the new environment. Most of the time your budgie is coming from a place where there were other birds, and he won't be used to the quiet. I always suggest playing budgie sounds to help your budgie feel more comfortable. It takes the bird three weeks to decompress, three weeks to learn your routine, and three months to feel really at home. Give your budgie the time he needs to become your friend."

JENNIFER TAYLOR,
Jennifer's budgies

> Be aware that many a small bird has been injured or killed by being stepped on or sat on. It happens. I've heard many a story about a very tame bird that was overlooked and killed that way. I've also heard far too many stories of birds flying out the door, never to be seen again. Don't fall prey to the 'my bird never flies off my shoulder' bit, because it only takes that one time. Even a clipped bird can fly great distances if it catches the wind just right."

ANITA GOLDEN,
formerly Nita's Nest

66 *It's good to remember that parrots, and that includes the tiniest budgie, are highly intelligent social creatures. We are asking a lot for them to be a part of our lives. We should do everything we can to provide opportunities to stimulate and mimic natural behaviors in captivity. A budgie is not going to be content with sitting in a cage, doing very little for the entirety of its life."*

SHANNON COCHRAN,
Chesapeake Aviary

66 *Budgies are little drama queens, so being excited with them helps them. Every day, provide your budgie with independent playtime (a play stand) as well as a couple of hours of your time. That includes riding on your shoulder while you do chores and sitting on the couch, watching TV with the bird. They love the interaction."*

JANET L BERUBE,
The Parrot and Bird Emporium

CHAPTER 3

Preparing for Your Budgie

Setting up the Cage

Sizing

Plan to set up the cage before you bring your budgie home, and put it in a location where your budgie will be able to see other family members pass by from time to time throughout the day. Being whisked away from familiar surroundings and traveling to your home in a small cage or box is a stressful experience for a small bird, and your budgie will feel relieved when you place him in a comfortable cage with fresh food and water, several perches, and a few toys. As he settles into his new home, give him some time to decompress and get used to the new sights and sounds without a lot of human interaction. For the first couple of days, slowly approach the cage a few times each day and speak softly and reassuringly to your budgie so he can start getting acquainted with you.

The cage will likely be the most expensive item you buy for your budgie, so choose wisely and get one that is designed to last for many years. Get the best-quality cage you can afford, and select the largest one that will fit within the space you have available. Be guided by function rather than fashion, so don't allow yourself to be distracted by antique or ornate cages. Not every bird cage is appropriate for budgies, and not every pet store stocks cages that are specifically designed for these birds. Fortunately for the first-time budgie owner, there are now a number of

pet supply companies that sell their products online, so if your local pet store or breeder cannot provide you with a budgie cage that meets your needs, consider shopping for one on the Internet.

Budgies are active birds, and they need room to hop around and flap their wings when they aren't engaged in free-flight exercise outside of the cage. A single budgie requires a cage that is about 18 inches wide, long, and tall. Two birds need a larger cage that is about 24 to 30 inches wide, long, and tall. Budgies like to climb, so the cage should have a number of horizontal bars they can hold onto with their feet and beak as they move up and down the sides of the cage. The bars should be spaced no more than half an inch apart so that inquisitive birds can't accidentally stick their heads through the bars and get stuck. Don't buy a cage with rubber or plastic coating on the bars because it can be chewed off and swallowed.

The cage should have a door that is large enough for the bird to enter freely and for you to insert your hand when necessary. Bird cages usually feature one of three basic door styles. One of the more common doors

slides open when you push it up from the bottom. Unfortunately, an active budgie can also push open this style of door from inside the cage, and the door can suddenly drop back down again and cause an injury to the bird's neck. If you buy a cage with this type of door, get a small snap hook from the hardware store that you can use to latch the door shut. Doors that swing open from the side and doors that open at the top and pull down like a drawbridge are better options. The drawbridge-style door can also provide a convenient place for your budgie to land when returning to the cage.

Food and water dishes usually come with the cage, but if you will keep two budgies in one cage, consider buying a second set of dishes to prevent squabbles. Put several wood perches in the cage to give your pet comfortable places to roost. Choosing perches of different widths will help your bird maintain healthy feet. Pine dowels allow budgies to safely fill their desire to chew on something, but you can also buy or make your own perches from tree branches, and the twisted shapes will look more natural than wooden dowels. Branches from apple, elm, manzanita, and willow trees are nontoxic to budgies, but you must be certain that the tree hasn't been sprayed with insecticides or other chemicals. You can also include a perch made of rope to add variety, but be sure to trim any loose strands of fiber that appear if your budgie gnaws on the rope perch. These loose strings can get caught on a toe or twist around a foot and cause injury. And if your budgie appears to be eating the fibers, remove the rope perch and replace it with a wooden one. Another essential item is a bird

DID YOU KNOW?

Extra Vertebrae

Though small, budgies have more vertebrae in their necks than humans. These extra vertebrae enable budgies to turn their heads nearly 180 degrees. On the other hand, humans are capable of only a 90-degree rotation.

bath, and pet stores offer a variety to choose from. Budgies enjoy bathing in shallow water, and if you don't provide them with a separate bird bath they may bathe in their water dish and splash out the water.

Temperature and environment control

It's important to choose the right location for your budgie's cage. Place the cage in an area of your home where the temperature doesn't fluctuate wildly and where heating and air conditioning vents don't blow directly onto the cage. Ideally, the room temperature should stay around 70 to 75 degrees Fahrenheit, but the birds will feel comfortable within a temperature range of 60 to 85 degrees Fahrenheit.

Budgies enjoy interacting with their human family members through-out the day, so place the cage where your bird can frequently see them, but not in a high-traffic area where excess noise and activity may make him feel anxious. Birds feel more secure when at least one side of their cage is against a wall, and an even better location is a bright corner of a room where two sides of the cage will be next to a wall. Don't put the cage in front of a window, where temperatures can change rapidly and outside sights and sounds can scare your bird. For similar reasons, you should not put the cage in a kitchen or bathroom because fumes from cleaning products and the continual temperature and humidity changes in these rooms can make your bird ill.

INFO BOX

Necessary Supplies

Misty Maruska & Melody Maruska, Parrots N Stuff

The full setup for your new budgie will typically be the biggest expense, but it is so important to know the care necessary and provide that for your new bird. Basic supplies are sometimes overlooked or undercut for what your budgie really needs to be healthy and happy.

Cage: Should be at least 18 x 18. Oftentimes stores will sell much smaller cages. Budgies are very active, and they need enough room to play and move about.

Toys: I hear people talk about how they will only buy hard, indestructible toys for their bird because they don't want more mess than they have to have. This mindset will only hurt your bird in the long run. We recommend starting with at least three to four toys of all different types. Get a toy that is noisy and jingly, a toy that has wood to chew, a toy with soft wood, grasses, or other materials that can be easily destroyed, and a foraging toy. This will give your bird the entertainment it needs for self-entertainment while you are away or unable to interact directly.

Perches: Most cages come with basic plastic or wooden dowels, which are fine short term. In order to ensure good

INFO BOX

Necessary Supplies

foot health, though, you really want to focus on different types and styles—wood, rope, concrete, different shapes, sizes, etc.

Food: *Oftentimes budgies are sent home with standard budgie seed. This is okay when they are young, but it is not a sustainable, healthy diet long term, although a lot of people, stores, and companies still encourage it. Keep in mind that it is important to buy the food the bird is used to, and then slowly transition the budgie to something healthier. During transitions to new homes, not all budgies do well, and they need their comfort food to help them adjust without too much weight loss. Variety is key: the more fresh fruits and vegetables the better, but not all birds will take to them. Specialty stores typically carry a variety of food with different ingredients, even for the pickiest of birds, and they can help get your new budgie on the right track for a long, healthy life.*

Cuttlebone & Mineral Block: *A lot of people never realize their birds need these supplements. The birds may not utilize them for weeks or months, but having the supplements available is necessary to ensure budgies get what they need, especially if it is a female, as they have the ability to lay eggs without a mate.*

INFO BOX

Necessary Supplies

Kitchen/Ounce Scale: I buy mine from our local grocery stores. This is not vital but can come in handy and give you tremendous peace of mind when bringing home a new bird. Weighing your bird every couple of days during the adjust- ment period is a good idea. The biggest problem we see with baby birds going home is that typically they are used to being in a cage with other birds. You then separate them, and they don't eat as well because they are flock birds. Eat with your bird as though he's a part of your flock! Don't panic if there is a small weight loss. A couple of grams is okay. Just make sure the bird's weight stops going down and then maintains!

Spray Bottle/Mister: It is vital to bathe your bird as most birds do not sufficiently bathe themselves. Having a spray bottle or mister on hand will help you get in the habit of frequently misting your bird.

Keeping the cage clean

Dirty cages can lead to serious health problems, so it is important to keep your budgie's home clean. Line the bottom of the cage with paper that is absorbent enough to soak up the liquid in the droppings, and replace the paper at least once each week. Newsprint is now free of lead, so discarded newspapers work well for this purpose. Don't use the sand- paper cage liners sold in pet stores because birds can eat the sand and develop gastrointestinal problems. Remove the food and water bowls each day and wash them with a mild detergent to inhibit the growth of bacteria. After washing, rinse and dry the bowls before replacing them in the cage. You can spot clean messy surfaces in the cage with a damp rag when necessary, including perches and toys.

Clean the cage about once a month. Scrub the perches, and clean and rotate the toys. Also, wash the tray at the bottom of the cage, and replace the paper after the tray has dried. Be sure to use nontoxic cleaning products. A one-part vinegar to one-part water solution makes a good disinfectant, and you can use baking soda to scrub surfaces that need something a little more abrasive.

About once every six months, give the cage a more thorough cleaning. To do this, you will need to let your budgie out of the cage for some

Photo Courtesy of
Maureen Milton

supervised flying time or temporarily move him to an alternate cage. Remove the food and water dishes, the perches, and the toys, and take the cage outside or place it in a bathtub or shower. Wash the cage completely, and focus attention on any areas where droppings tend to accumulate. Also, wash the food and water dishes, the perches, and the toys, and let them dry completely before putting them back in the cage and returning your bird to his home.

Toys for the cage

Wild budgies occupy much of their time searching for food and out-maneuvering predators. In captivity, they need a variety of toys to stay active and mentally stimulated. Budgies love swings, bells, mirrors, and ladders. Provide your bird with an assortment of toys, and rotate them to different locations around the cage. Bells should not be round with small openings that can trap a bird's foot or toe. Choose small bells that have a clapper and a wide opening at the bottom.

Regularly inspect toys to make sure they are still safe, and discard those with broken, sharp, or loose parts. Check ropes for loose strands that can entangle your budgie, and trim the strings or replace the toy. Dispose of toys with a plastic or metallic coating that begins to flake or peel off. Although mirrors are fun, interactive toys, single birds can sometimes focus too much attention on their own reflections and pay less attention to you. If that begins to happen, you should remove the mirror until your bird begins to pay more attention to you and its training.

Photo Courtesy of
Alisha Morton

Ask the Experts!

Getting the Right Supplies

New budgie owners should be well-prepared with the right supplies to ensure their bird's health and happiness. Necessary items include a variety of toys for mental and physical stimulation, natural wood perches of different sizes to promote foot health, and a spacious cage to accommodate these items and allow for flight and exercise. Additionally, a nutritionally balanced diet, including fresh foods and quality seed or pellet mixes, is crucial. Providing a cuttlebone and mineral block can help meet calcium and mineral needs, especially for females. Understanding these requirements and the reasoning behind them can greatly improve the quality of life for the budgie.

" *Many people new to birds and budgies may opt for brightly colored plastic toys. While that's not all bad ... budgies, being parrots, need appropriate foraging and enrichment opportunities. Providing their daily intake of food within items like this will help keep them occupied."*

SHANNON COCHRAN,
Chesapeake Aviary

" *You will need some extra feed cups other than the usual pair supplied with the cage. In addition to food and water, you will want a cup for supplemental foods. I normally feed a good seed mix but also supply pellets in a separate dish. Place a cuttlebone and perhaps a mineral block inside the cage as well. You don't need a cage cover, especially if your cage is not kept near a bright light, but if you do use a cover, it's important to use it consistently."*

ANITA GOLDEN,
Formerly Nita's Nest

" *You will need an adequate size cage with lots of toys they can shred. Toys are very important for budgies' well-being. They need to shred and tear. Also, they need a play stand ... There should be a variety of perches in different sizes and textures."*

JANET L BERUBE,
The Parrot and Bird Emporium

Choosing the Right Budgie

One or two?

How much time you have available to spend with your budgie each day is an important consideration when deciding whether to adopt one, two, or more birds. Budgies can get bored and unhappy if they are left alone in a cage. In addition to providing mental stimulation, having a budgie partner can also help both birds maintain their physical health as they groom each other while socializing. If the time you have available to play and socialize with your bird is somewhat limited, and you are out of the house for much of the day, consider adopting two birds so they can play together and entertain each other when you're not home. You also might find that you really enjoy watching the two birds interacting with each other.

On the other hand, two budgies tend to bond more closely with each other than with their human family members, which can make them a little more difficult to train and less inclined to imitate human speech. This doesn't mean that the two birds will ignore you altogether, but it may take more time to train them and teach them to speak. One way to reduce the negative aspects of keeping two birds is to adopt one bird at a time. This will allow your first bird to receive some basic training and form a bond with you. After three or four months,

HELPFUL TIP

Green or Blue?

Wild budgies are usually light green with yellow faces, but there are many recognized color combinations in domestic members of this species. For example, blue budgies occur when yellow pigmentation is absent, allowing the blue coloring to show through. Other budgie colors can range from olive to mauve, to cobalt, to white. Budgies may also have unique markings and striping patterns. One popular striping pattern is cinnamon, which occurs when a budgie's markings are brown rather than black. One of the rarest budgie color mutations is the rainbow mutation, which results in a yellow-faced blue series opaline clearwing.

your budgie will have become attached to you, and you can then adopt a companion bird. When you bring a second bird home, it's important to quarantine the new bird for at least 30 days before introducing it to your resident bird. This quarantine period helps ensure that the new bird doesn't have any health issues that may not be immediately apparent, protecting your existing bird from potential illnesses. Keep the new bird in a separate room during this time to prevent any chance of disease transmission. After the quarantine period, you can start the introduction process by keeping the birds in separate cages near each other so they can get acquainted. Gradually, you can slowly introduce them in a neutral space, such as a room where they can fly around together under your supervision.

Male or female?

Should you adopt a male or a female budgie? Males and females both make excellent pets, but there are some differences in behavior between the two. Males are sometimes more friendly, and they tend to be more inclined to speak. Females can also form a strong attachment to their owners, and they can be taught to speak, but they are usually not as vocal and may not speak as clearly. Once they reach full maturity, female budgies may also display a more forceful personality and be more protective of their home.

It is sometimes difficult to determine the sex of an adult budgie before it is a year old. In general, the color of the cere is the best way to determine the bird's sex. Males have a solid blue or lavender cere, the fleshy part of the beak around the nostrils. Females have a white or brown cere, which can darken as they age.

What color?

Budgies come in a spectacular array of colors and patterns, and which color you choose is entirely up to you. Larger pet stores usually have a selection of birds in various shades of yellow, green, blue, and gray. Although some birds that were selectively bred for rare color variations may be more susceptible to health problems, it is unlikely that you will find these birds in a pet store. So, feel free to choose any healthy bird that appeals to your own color preferences. The budgie's color will not make a difference to its quality as a companion.

Breeder or pet store

A healthy budgie should be active and have bright, clear eyes. Unless it is the budgie's usual naptime, the bird should not be sitting still with its head buried in its feathers. Budgies are usually available at most large pet stores, and reputable stores should be able to guarantee the health of the bird for at least the first few days or weeks, which is long enough for you to take the bird to an avian veterinarian for an initial health check-up. A bird purchased at a pet store will be less expensive than one bought from a breeder. On the downside, pet store budgies have usually spent much of their lives in an aviary with other birds instead of humans, so it might initially take you more time to train the bird and get it to trust you.

Depending on where you live, it might also be possible for you to buy a bird directly from a breeder. You can search online for a local budgie breeder. A hand-raised budgie or a young budgie that is already used to being handled will cost more, but it will be easier for you to train and will likely bond with you more quickly.

Budgies are also sometimes available for adoption from local animal shelters and bird rescue organizations.

Ask the Experts!

Choosing the right budgie

Selecting the right budgie involves considering the bird's age, personality, and background. Preferably, one should purchase from a breeder because they can provide detailed information about the bird's health, upbringing, and personality. Young birds that are hand-fed and raised with human interaction are generally friendlier and easier to tame. In contrast, pet stores, especially large chains, often lack detailed histories of their birds and may not offer post-purchase support.

I strongly advise not only going through a breeder but getting a bird as young as possible after it is weaned. Pet store birds, especially from 'big box' stores, are raised in quantity without much human interaction. It is difficult to know how old they are when they arrive at the pet store as well as when you buy them."

SUSAN M. ANDRESEN,
Bull City budgies

"Choosing the right budgie varies from person to person. Some people choose by color, some by gender, and some by personality. Going through a breeder to get your budgie has many advantages. You get to ask questions about the budgie (age, gender, diet, personality). Birds that come from a breeder are usually more friendly, especially if they're hand-fed."

JENNIFER TAYLOR,

Jennifer's budgies

"There is quite a difference in a hand-tamed or hand-fed budgie, or a budgie who has had neither of those. Hand-fed/handled budgies are more human-oriented. They were worked with in a way that taught them to bond and appreciate humans. If budgies are not handled/hand-fed, it just means that the parents of the bird did 100% of the work, and the bird has never really been handled or worked with. Some people choose to get just any budgie regardless of its upbringing, and some people are successful, but especially if you are a first-time bird owner, I would say that 90% of the time it is a disappointment, and the quality of bird you were hoping for is never achieved regardless of the amount of work you put into the bird."

MISTY MARUSKA & MELODY MARUSKA,

Parrots N Stuff

"When shopping for a budgie, going directly to a breeder is the best choice. They can often provide pretty accurate sexing on babies versus trying to do so on your own and getting it wrong. A good breeder will be there to help at any step of the way and will provide support to their customers if needed."

SHANNON COCHRAN,

Chesapeake Aviary

"I would recommend finding a pet through a breeder, and especially one that hand feeds their babies. You will then start out with a bird that's already tame for the most part, and one who is certainly unafraid of humans. If you must buy from a pet shop, look for a very young bird that still has stripes across the forehead. You will have more luck in taming a young bird."

ANITA GOLDEN,

formerly Nita's Nest

" *Personality will be difficult to determine in a store, and you will be at the mercy of luck. To stack the odds in your favor, you should try to pick out a boy. Female budgies that have exceptionally good person-alities make good pets. I know of many people who lucked out and had wonderful female pet budgies. But as a rule, the average run-of-the-mill male budgie will have a better pet-type personality than the average female budgie. And the outliers with poor personalities are more often going to be female than male. This is not because females have bad personalities. It's because the role of the female in bird life is not the same as what people are looking for in a pet bird. The role of the male just naturally fits better for what people want as a pet."*

DIANA WILKEWITZ,
Budgiedin Budgerigars

" *Honestly, finding the 'right' budgie implies there may be a 'wrong' budgie. I don't agree with this. Like people, every single bird has its own personality. And like people, you can't tell a baby's personality when it's a baby. In fact, the way the baby is raised determines what kind of per-son they will be. Same with budgies. Color mutation, sex/gender, and age have nothing to do with how sweet or personable a budgie will be. Clutch size, upbringing and environment, and daily interaction and socialization with humans is what shapes them, nurtures them, and brings out their 'true' personality."*

LESLIE CORYN,
Featherbelle Aviary

CHAPTER 4

A Healthy Budgie

Healthy Diet

Seed and pellets

You want your budgie to have the best life possible, and proper nutrition is essential for your bird's health and longevity. Like humans, budgies require a balanced diet that includes protein, fat, carbohydrates, vitamins, and minerals. Start with the same basic diet of seeds or pellets

that the pet store or breeder was feeding your budgie. If possible, continue using the same brand of packaged birdseed or pellets that your bird is accustomed to eating, and avoid making dietary changes until he has had time to settle into his new home. Later, you can adjust your budgie's menu by gradually introducing pellets or replacing pellets with seed to create the balanced diet that you prefer or that the veterinarian recommends.

Whether you feed your budgie a seed-based diet or pellet-based diet, it's important to recognize that seeds and pellets alone do not provide all the nutrients he needs to stay healthy. In addition to seeds, wild budgies eat a variety of fruits, berries, seed sprouts, and green vegetation, depending on what is available during each season of the year. You can supplement your budgie's diet by serving him small portions of many of the same fruits, vegetables, and leafy greens that you enjoy.

Seeds

Seeds and grains have always played a significant role in meeting the budgie's dietary needs, both in the wild and in captivity. Seeds have the high-fat content that gives wild budgies the energy they need to fly from one area to another in their constant search for food and water. In captivity, however, budgies lead a much more sedentary life, and their diet must be adjusted accordingly. If your budgie is on a seed-based diet, mixed birdseed should make up about 50% of your bird's total food intake. Feed your budgie small portions of fresh fruit, vegetables, seed sprouts, and leafy greens to provide the other 50% of his nutritionally balanced diet. Pet stores offer a variety of packaged seed mixes that are specifically designed for budgies.

Don't buy a seed mix intended for wild birds because it will include seeds with a higher fat content than what is recommended for budgies. A quality seed mix for budgies will usually include canary grass seed, several varieties of millet, oat groats, niger seed, and flax seed. A single budgie will eat about a teaspoon and a half of seed each day, or about a pound of seed per month, so avoid buying large quantities of packaged seed that will be stored for several months. Over time, seeds can potentially lose much of their freshness and nutritional value before your budgie has a chance to eat them.

Top off the food dish with fresh seeds every day, and make certain your budgie is never without something to eat. Because budgies peel the husks from seeds before eating the kernels and let the empty husks fall back into the food dish, a layer of husks can form on the top of the dish and make it appear full of seeds when it really isn't. Before refilling the food dish, use a spoon to remove the empty husks, or simply hold the dish over a trash receptacle and blow off the husks before adding more seeds.

You can also sprout seeds from a packaged mix and offer them to your budgie as a nutritious treat. Sprouting triggers a biochemical reaction within seeds that often decreases the fat content while increasing the amount of available vitamins and other nutrients.

Pellets

A number of years ago, pet food companies began offering bird food in the form of small pellets that are formulated to meet the specific nutritional requirements of budgies and other bird species. Pellets are made from a combination of seeds, grains, fruits, vegetables, and other nutrients. Many veterinarians recommend a pellet-based diet for budgies to help prevent nutritional disorders. If your budgie is on a pellet-based diet, the pellets should represent about 75% of your bird's food intake. Feed your budgie small portions of fresh fruit, vegetables, seed sprouts, leafy greens, and mixed birdseed to provide the other 25% of your budgie's nutritionally balanced diet. Make sure the pellets you buy are formulated for budgies and contain natural ingredients. Avoid buying pellets that include preservatives and artificial dyes.

If you decide to switch your budgie from a seed-based diet to a pellet-based diet, and your budgie isn't accustomed to eating pellets, you will need to introduce the new diet gradually. Birds are often suspicious of anything new, and budgies sometimes refuse to eat pellets at first because they don't recognize them as food. Younger birds are usually more enthusiastic about trying new foods than older birds, and the amount of time required to transition a budgie from seed to pellets often varies from one bird to another; it usually takes a few weeks. Be patient, and never attempt to force a budgie to eat pellets by withholding other food because doing so will cause unnecessary stress and can quickly escalate to serious health problems.

There are several ways to help make the transition from seed to pellets easier. If your bird is very tame, you can try offering pellets as a treat or pretend to eat pellets yourself and then offer some to your budgie. Another way to introduce your budgie to pellets is to mix some pellets with his regular seed and monitor him to see if he actually eats them, or if he simply flicks them out of the food dish. If your budgie seems resistant to eating pellets, you might need to help him get used to the smell and taste of this unfamiliar food. Try crushing some pellets into a powder and sprinkling it over the seeds, vegetables, or fresh fruit that you usually feed him. A variation of this technique is to place some crushed pellets in the bottom of the food dish and add a small amount of warm water to soften them. After a few minutes, add the usual seeds to the food dish and press them down into the softened pellets before placing the dish back in the cage. As your budgie picks out the seeds, he will become familiar with the taste of the pellets.

Once your budgie begins to eat pellets, you can mix a small number of pellets with his usual seed and then gradually increase the ratio of pellets to seed. Start by feeding a mixture of 25% pellets and 75% seed for two weeks. If your budgie accepts his new diet and continues to eat normally, increase the ratio of pellets to seed by 25% every two weeks until you have successfully converted him from a seed-based diet to a pellet-based diet. Monitor your budgie carefully during each step of the transition from seed to pellets. If his droppings diminish, or if he stops eating his usual daily amount of pellets mixed with seeds, reduce the amount of pellets and add more seeds to his diet. Wait another two weeks before attempting to move on to the next step by increasing the ratio of pellets to seed.

Feeding schedule

Establishing a regular feeding schedule will help your budgie stay happy, active, and healthy. Budgies like routine and maintaining a consistent feeding schedule will reassure your companion that he can expect to receive food around the same time every day. Refill your budgie's food dish with seeds or pellets twice a day, once in the morning and again in the afternoon or early evening. Offer small portions of fresh vegetables every day or every other day to help balance your bird's nutritional needs. For added variety and to provide essential protein and calcium, serve your budgie small pieces of hard-boiled egg about once a week. Because fruits and berries contain more natural sugar than vegetables, serve small portions of fruit only two or three times a week. Bear in mind that it is normal for your budgie's droppings to become slightly more watery or loose after eating fruits and vegetables because these foods have a higher water content than seeds and pellets.

Water

Refill your budgie's water dish with fresh, clean water every day and more often if there are food particles or bird droppings in the water. Dirty water can harbor harmful bacteria that can make your bird sick, so it's a good idea to check the water dish occasionally to make sure the water is still clean. If your household tap water is safe for you to drink, it's probably safe for your budgie. Some budgie owners prefer to use filtered water or bottled drinking water because many water treatment facilities use chlorine and other chemicals to disinfect the water. Although water with low levels of chemical disinfectants is considered safe for humans to drink, it can be harmful to small birds. If your tap water is chlorinated, or if you are uncertain about the quality of the tap water in your area, use bottled, non-carbonated drinking water instead.

Vegetables and fruits

Fresh fruits and vegetables provide your budgie with the essential vitamins and nutrients that mixed birdseed and pellets alone do not supply. Your budgie will also enjoy sampling the various flavors and textures of these foods. Experiment with different ways to serve these fresh foods to see how your budgie prefers to eat them. Wild budgies are ground feeders, and your bird might like eating chopped fruit and vegetables served in a small dish on the bottom of the cage. Some birds also enjoy nibbling fruit wedges and leafy greens suspended from the top or attached to the side of the cage near a perch. Be sure to wash all fruits and vegetables before serving them to eliminate any traces of pesticides or chemical fertilizer. Also, remove seeds and pits before serving fruit because some are toxic. Dispose of uneaten fruit and vegetables after several hours to avoid spoilage.

Vegetables

Your budgie can eat the following vegetables:

- Alfalfa sprouts
- Beans (cooked)
- Broccoli
- Cabbage
- Carrots (and carrot greens)
- Cauliflower
- Cilantro
- Cucumber
- Endive
- Green beans
- Bell pepper
- Kale
- Mustard greens
- Mung bean sprouts
- Parsley
- Peas
- Potato (cooked)
- Pumpkin
- Radish
- Soybeans
- Spinach
- Squash
- Watercress
- Wheatgrass sprouts
- Yam
- Zucchini

Fruits

Your budgie can eat the following fruits and berries:

- ✓ Apples
- ✓ Bananas
- ✓ Blackberries
- ✓ Blueberries
- ✓ Cantaloupe
- ✓ Cherries
- ✓ Figs
- ✓ Grapes
- ✓ Guava
- ✓ Kiwi
- ✓ Mango
- ✓ Nectarines
- ✓ Oranges
- ✓ Papaya
- ✓ Peaches
- ✓ Pears
- ✓ Pineapple
- ✓ Plums
- ✓ Raspberries
- ✓ Strawberries
- ✓ Tangerines
- ✓ Watermelon

Calcium and trace minerals

Although a base diet of pellets or seeds and small servings of fresh fruit and vegetables will satisfy most of your budgie's nutritional requirements, he will still need some additional calcium and trace minerals. To complete his diet, place a cuttlefish bone or a mineral block inside the cage to provide these vital nutrients. A cuttlefish bone, or cuttlebone, is the internal shell of the cuttlefish, a close relative of the squid. Mineral blocks are artificially made by combining calcium, minerals, and other important nutrients in the form of a small round or rectangular block. Most mineral blocks and cuttlefish bones come with clips that allow you to attach them to the inside of the cage near a perch where your budgie can access them. Cuttlefish bones have a hard side and a soft side and must be installed with the soft side facing the interior of the cage. Don't

worry if your budgie seldom shows interest in the cuttlefish bone or mineral block; he will occasionally nibble on it whenever he needs to.

Do not offer your budgie grit as a mineral supplement. Budgies do not need grit to help them digest their food because they remove the husks before swallowing seeds, so there is little indigestible material in their diet. Some budgies overindulge in grit when it is provided, and this can result in gastrointestinal tract obstruction.

Unhealthy foods

Although many of the same foods that you enjoy are also safe for your budgie, some foods are potentially toxic. Here is a list of foods that you should never allow your budgie to eat:

Alcohol: Do not allow your budgie to sip alcoholic beverages. Alcohol is toxic to birds and can cause death.

Avocado: The avocado plant contains a fungicidal toxin called *persin*. When ingested by a bird, persin can cause heart damage, respiratory difficulty, weakness, and sudden death.

Dried beans: Many dry, uncooked beans contain proteins called *lectins* that are highly toxic to birds. However, when beans are thoroughly cooked, they are a healthy food that budgies can safely enjoy.

Caffeine: Never allow your budgie to sip coffee, tea, or caffeinated beverages. Very small amounts of caffeine can increase heart rate, trigger arrhythmia, or cause cardiac arrest in birds.

Chocolate: Even small amounts of chocolate can cause vomiting, increase heart rate, induce seizures, and cause death in birds.

Fruit seeds: Always remove the seeds before serving fruit to your budgie. The seeds of many common fruits contain trace amounts of a toxic cyanide compound.

Junk food: Never offer your bird a bite of salty, fatty, or sugary foods, such as potato chips, French fries, or pretzels. Salt and sugar can disrupt the electrolyte and fluid balance in your budgie's tiny body, and the effects can be deadly.

Onions and garlic: Although these vegetables are healthy for people to consume, they contain chemical compounds that are toxic to birds and can irritate the lining of the mouth, esophagus, and crop, causing ulcers.

Rhubarb: The oxalic acid found in rhubarb can cause severe irritation to a bird's digestive system.

FUN FACT
Budgie Vision

Budgies have a unique way of seeing the world called monocular vision. This trait means that budgies can move each eye independently, unlike humans, who have binocular vision and use both eyes simultaneously. In addition, monocular vision allows budgies to observe areas on each side of their body, increasing their range of vision. As a result, not only can budgies see more than humans, but their eyesight is also much better than ours.

Photo Courtesy of
Alisha Morton

Ask the Experts!

Nutritional advice

Proper nutrition is crucial for a budgie's health. New owners may not realize the importance of a balanced diet, which includes a variety of foods. While seed mixes are common, they should not be the bird's sole food source. Incorporating pellets, fresh fruits, and vegetables can provide the necessary vitamins and minerals. Also, the diet should be adjusted based on the bird's age, health, and activity level. Monitoring food intake and offering a diverse range of foods can help prevent nutritional deficiencies and promote a healthier life for the budgie.

" *Some believe that pellets are the only way to go, forgetting that pellets are ground-up seeds with filler and vitamins. Some believe a high-quality seed mix is the way to go. I think we can all agree on the fact that fresh food chop, a mixture of chopped up fruits and veggies, is essential to your bird's diet. A sprinkle of flax, chia, or hemp seed on top makes for a more complete meal. Start introducing your budgie to fresh food as soon as you bring the bird home. The budgie might not eat it right away, but continue to offer it, as this is essential to the bird's diet."*

LESLIE CORYN,
Featherbelle Aviary

" *The biggest myth I see in regards to nutrition is that pellets are the best thing you can offer your parrot and that seed is junk food. It's just not true. Pellets are heat-treated and offer very little nutrients besides covering the bases for your bird's vitamin and mineral intake. Seed is not junk food. Budgies are primarily grass-seed eaters in the wild. Finding a well-rounded, quality seed mix that contains dried fruits, veggies, and pellets, as well as offering fresh food items such as greens, steamed sweet potato, sprouts, apple, etc., can improve the health of your budgie. Budgies aren't very big fresh eaters overall since they are grass parakeets, but it is always a good idea to start researching how to incorporate fresh food items into your bird's diet."*

SHANNON COCHRAN,
Chesapeake Aviary

" *Most seed mixes marketed for parakeets nowadays contain small colored pellets which most birds do not eat. Buy a good, straight seed mix for parakeets and supplement it with leafy greens, broccoli, etc. Many birds won't eat these at first, but keep putting a little in the cage so they can get familiar with it, or have some on your dinner plate if the bird is out during your meals. Do not buy large quantities of seed at one time as it will lose its nutritional value before it is eaten. Store excess seed in the freezer. Budgies eat approximately a pound of seed/month or less, so buy accordingly.*"

SUSAN M. ANDRESEN,

Bull City budgies

" *Offer your budgie fresh fruit and vegetables. Just because they don't like it one day doesn't mean they won't like it another day. Sprinkle the fruit/veggies with seed to encourage them to try it.*"

JENNIFER TAYLOR,

Jennifer's budgies

Interaction

Time outside the cage

In addition to a balanced diet, your budgie needs regular exercise to stay trim and healthy. Wild budgies spend much of their time flying, climbing, and foraging for food. After your budgie is tame and accustomed to his new cage and surroundings, you can allow him to play and exercise outside the cage. This will help keep your budgie in good physical condition, and the more time he spends in supervised activities outside the cage, the more interested he will be in interacting with you and other family members.

The amount of time you allow your budgie to exercise outside the cage will largely depend on the time you have available. Try to provide at least two 15-minute exercise sessions each day. If possible, increase the time your budgie is allowed outside the cage to one or two hours each day. Monitor your bird, and if he starts breathing heavily during vigorous exercise, allow him to stop and catch his breath before continuing. Flying is the most natural exercise for birds, and it helps improve their cardiovascular health, muscle strength, and respiratory function. Before you let your budgie fly outside the cage, make sure the room is safe and secure:

HEALTH ALERT
Blood Loss

Due to the diminutive size of budgies, they have a small volume of blood. Therefore, losing only a dozen drops of blood could prove fatal for these birds. If your bird experiences bleeding due to trauma, it's crucial to apply pressure with sterile gauze to the area and seek immediate veterinary care if the bleeding continues.

Windows and doors: Keep all windows and doors closed. Even well-trained budgies will fly out of an open door or window, and once outdoors, they are usually impossible to recapture.

Fans: Turn off all fans, including ceiling fans. Budgies cannot see fan blades in motion, and they can sustain serious injuries if they fly into them.

Mirrors: Remove or cover any mirrors in the room. Pet birds fly into mirrors and injure themselves because they perceive them as open space rather than solid objects.

Electrical cords: Hide or unplug any electrical cords in the room. Your budgie will be tempted to nibble on exposed electrical cords, which can create a potential fire hazard and may expose your bird to electric shock.

Standing water: Budgies are attracted to water, and they can drown while exploring the water in open toilet bowls or the standing water in sinks and bathtubs.

Encouraging your budgie to dance is another way to help him exercise outside the cage. Birds naturally respond to sound, and many budgies react to music by bobbing their heads up and down and moving their feet to the rhythm. Budgies seem to prefer lively music with a medium tempo, including pop and reggae tunes. Listen to a variety of music with your bird to find out what he likes and see if he begins to sway or move around. If he does, praise him and offer him a treat to encourage his inner dancer. If he seems a bit reluctant to start dancing on his own, demonstrate how fun it can be by moving in time with the music or by showing him videos of other birds dancing. As your budgie makes progress, continue to praise him and offer treats, and before long, he will start dancing whenever you play one of his favorite songs.

Human interaction

Budgies are naturally playful and affectionate, and they enjoy receiving affection from their human owners. Because kissing is a common way for humans to show affection, it might seem perfectly natural to kiss your budgie on the beak. But while giving your budgie a quick kiss on the top of the head is unlikely to do any harm, kissing a budgie near the beak can transfer harmful bacteria to your bird that can cause serious illness. Bacteria are generally classified as either gram-positive or gram-negative based on the different types of cell walls they have. The naturally occurring bacteria in the gastrointestinal tract of birds are primarily gram-positive, while the naturally occurring bacteria in the gastrointestinal tract of humans and other mammals are primarily gram-negative.

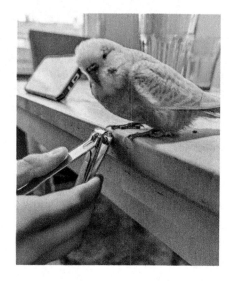

No matter how clean your mouth is, your saliva can still carry many types of bacteria that the avian immune system is not prepared to defend itself against. If some of these bacteria are transferred to your budgie, he could potentially develop a life-threatening respiratory or gastrointestinal tract infection. To avoid exposing your budgie to the harmful bacteria in your saliva, don't offer him food that you have already taken

a bite out of, and resist the urge to kiss your budgie on the beak. Better ways to show your budgie that you care are hand-feeding him spray millet or another healthy treat or softly stroking him under the throat or on the back of the head and neck.

Avoiding toxic interaction

Your budgie will enjoy regular exercise and flight time outside the cage, but make certain you keep him safe from common household items that are toxic to birds. Budgies are very curious, and they often nibble on things as they investigate their surroundings. Don't leave medicines for humans or other pets lying around where an inquisitive budgie can chew or swallow them. Birds are also sometimes attracted to the smell and taste of mouse and rat poison, so if you use pesticides, be sure to keep them where your bird can't find them.

Are there houseplants in your home? While some common houseplants are safe, others are dangerous for birds, such as those in the philodendron family. Don't allow your budgie to have access to houseplants unless you are certain they are safe. You can perform an online search to find out whether a specific houseplant is safe or unsafe for budgies. A general list of plants that are known to be poisonous to pets is available on the Oregon Veterinary Medical Association website at https://oregonvma.org/care-health/safety/poisonous-plants.

Because birds have very sensitive respiratory systems, the fumes from many household products are toxic to budgies. These include perfumes, air fresheners, scented candles, hairspray, insecticides, mothballs, household cleaning products, and fumes from drying paint, varnish, and adhesives. Avoid using products that contain toxic chemicals around your budgie, and keep him in another room if you must use a product but are unsure if it can be safely used around birds. A less obvious source of fumes that are extremely toxic to budgies and other birds is nonstick cookware, which is often coated with a synthetic polymer called polytetrafluoroethylene (PTFE). A wide variety of kitchen products are manufactured with this nonstick coating, including frying pans, deep fryers, broiler pans, griddles, electric skillets, waffle makers, sheet pans, and kitchen utensils.

Although nonstick cookware is generally considered safe around humans, when heated to higher temperatures, PTFE coatings release airborne toxins that cause severe respiratory distress to birds, and sudden death often occurs shortly after exposure. If you must continue to use nonstick cookware, use only low to moderate heat, make certain the kitchen area is well-ventilated, and always keep your bird in another room away from the kitchen while cooking. However, the only way to completely eliminate the threat of PTFE poisoning is to remove nonstick cookware products from the kitchen.

Doctors warn people about the dangers of tobacco smoke, but smoke and nicotine are even more detrimental to birds. Cigarette smoke releases airborne toxins that will make your budgie susceptible to respiratory infections and disease. Birds absorb nicotine through their skin and feathers, which can cause an inflammation of the feet called "bumblefoot" and may lead to destructive behaviors such as feather plucking and biting at the legs and feet.

Ask the Experts!

Handling and Safety

Handling a budgie properly and safely letting it out of its enclosure are important for its well-being and trust-building with the owner. Gradual acclimatization to human interaction, ensuring the bird feels secure during handling, and creating a safe environment for it to explore outside the cage are crucial. Owners should start with gentle, consistent interaction to build trust and allow the budgie to become comfortable with being handled. Safety measures, like covering windows and mirrors, and supervising the bird during out-of-cage time, are essential to prevent accidents.

Begin with your new budgie in a small room that can be easily darkened, such as a bathroom. Work with the room almost dark to keep the bird calm at first. Move slowly and talk quietly. Gradually accustom the bird to your hand, and slowly remove the budgie from the cage. When the budgie seems at ease on your hand, walk around with the bird in the small room. To increase safety, I trim baby budgies' wings just enough to slow them down until they have learned where windows are so they don't crash into them too hard."

SUSAN M. ANDRESEN,
Bull City budgies

Some people do not agree with wing clipping, but I am a firm believer in it. I always clip a small amount and then test the bird to see how well it flies. The goal is to let the bird fly, but not gain altitude. A steady, slow descent is the perfect clip. This will keep them from flying so fast they may smash into a wall or window and get hurt, and it also serves to make them just a bit helpless and eager to have their human rescue them from the floor by allowing them to step up onto a hand or finger. It will greatly aid in taming the bird and keeping it tame. Just remember to clip in very small steps so you don't overdo it and end up with a bird that drops like a rock!"

ANITA GOLDEN,
formerly Nita's Nest

> *Always go slow. When letting your budgie out of its cage for the first few times, make sure all windows and mirrors are covered so the bird doesn't fly into them and get hurt. Once your budgie knows the lay of the land, you can uncover things."*

JENNIFER TAYLOR,

Jennifer's Budgies

> *When handling your budgie, never use force unless you absolutely have to for the bird's safety/immediate medical restraint. Work on building a relationship with your bird. Let it make good choices and reward the budgies for that (millet is usually a big hit!). New budgies may not want to come out immediately. Open the door and let them do so on their own. Just make sure the environment is safe."*

SHANNON COCHRAN,

Chesapeake Aviary

> *Playing with/handling your bird is important from day one. If you let the budgie adjust for too long, leaving it in the cage, the birds tend to regress and get even more hand-shy. Start from day one with handling and interacting. Make sure to give the bird plenty of time in the cage to sleep, eat, etc., but play away, and start bonding with your new addition!"*

MISTY MARUSKA & MELODY MARUSKA,

Parrots N Stuff

> *Make sure that the blinds are down/curtains closed when letting your budgie out of the cage. You might also want to cover any large mirrors. Make sure windows have screens and doors are closed. Offer your budgie a separate play stand where he/she can play independently. Budgies should feel comfortable stepping up on your finger in any situation. This way you can safely return your budgie to the cage."*

DIANE P HYDE,

Long Island Parrot Society

Typical Budgie Behavior

Common behaviors

One of the many reasons budgies have become such popular pets is that people enjoy watching them play and interact with each other. Although every bird has its own unique personality, all budgies will occasionally display the following typical behaviors when they are happy and healthy.

Stretching: After a period of rest, budgies often stretch their muscles just like many other animals. It's common to see a budgie first stretch a leg and wing on one side and then stretch the other leg and wing before finishing up by raising both wings together.

Fluffing feathers: Before going to sleep or before starting a new task, your budgie may fluff and shake out his feathers to make himself comfortable.

Resting on one leg: Budgies sometimes rest on one leg if it feels comfortable to them, and they may even go to sleep that way.

Head tucking: Some budgies like to sleep with their head tucked in the fluffed-up feathers on their back.

Head bobbing: Male budgies bob their heads up and down as part of their courtship display, and females will also participate in this behavior. When they are happy and excited, males also sometimes bob their heads in response to other males, toys, and even humans.

Regurgitating: Budgie parents regurgitate food to feed their chicks, and adult budgies will regurgitate food for their mates and companions of the same sex. Budgies may also regurgitate food for humans they are especially fond of.

Chewing: It's natural for budgies to chew and shred things to occupy their time and maintain their beaks. Safe types of wood you can provide your budgie to chew on include apple, balsa wood, bamboo, elm, eucalyptus, manzanita, maple, and pine. Make sure any wood you offer your budgie has not been coated with wood stain or finish and has not been sprayed with fertilizer or insecticide.

Ringing bells: Budgies enjoy their toys, and because a bell will move around and make noise when it is tapped, it can soon become a favorite plaything. If your budgie's interest in a bell becomes obsessive, it may indicate that your bird needs to spend more time interacting with you or he needs a budgie companion.

Eye pinning: Like other members of the parrot family, budgies sometimes rapidly dilate and constrict the pupils of their eyes when they are excited or especially interested in something.

Yawning and sneezing: Like humans, budgies yawn when they are about to fall asleep or when they have engaged in a lot of activity during the day. They also sneeze to clear their nasal passages.

Preening and grooming: Several times a day, budgies use their beaks to preen their feathers and waterproof them with oil from the uropygial gland at the base of the tail. When two birds are together, they will groom each other, often focusing attention on the head and chin areas that an individual bird can't reach on its own.

Vet visits

Finding a vet

Like other pets, your budgie should have annual health check-ups with a veterinarian. Wild birds instinctively hide signs of illness to avoid appearing weak and attracting the attention of predators, and pet birds typically follow the same pattern of concealing ill health. A veterinarian can often detect early signs of illness before it becomes a more serious problem. Regular check-ups also allow the vet to keep records of your budgie's health history, which will make it easier to recognize health

Photo Courtesy of
Samantha Stone

and nutritional issues if they arise later on. Ideally, choose a veterinarian before you purchase your budgie, and schedule an appointment for your bird's first examination on the day you bring him home to ensure that he is healthy.

Although most veterinary students study a variety of animal species, and many veterinarians have at least some familiarity with birds, a bird's anatomy and physiology are very different from that of dogs and cats. Whenever possible, it is best to find an avian veterinarian, one who specializes in the care and treatment of birds. There are several resources available to help you find an avian veterinarian in your area. The American Board of Veterinary Practitioners (ABVP) maintains a searchable list of avian veterinarians. You can use the search tool on their website at https://www.abvp.com/diplomate by clicking the "Find A Specialist" button, or you can call the ABVP at (800) 697-3583 to inquire about board-certified avian veterinarians in your vicinity. The Association of Avian Veterinarians (AAV) also has a searchable list of avian veterinarians. You can use the search tool on their website at https://www.aav.org by clicking the "Find a Vet" button, or you can call the AAV at (720) 458-4111 to ask if there are members in your area. In addition, the Lafeber Company provides a helpful veterinarian search tool on their website at https://lafeber.com/pet-birds/find-an-avian-vet. By entering your city and state and selecting an appropriate search radius, you can locate nearby veterinarians who practice avian medicine.

Another way to narrow your search for an avian veterinarian is to ask bird owners, breeders, and pet stores whom they would recommend. If you cannot find an avian veterinarian in your locale, you can still try contacting local veterinary practices to ask if someone in their office has experience with birds. Although some veterinarians don't specialize in birds, they might have many years of experience treating and caring for them.

Once you find a local veterinarian, call the office and ask for an appointment to meet the veterinarian. This will give you an opportunity to ask a few questions about the veterinary practice and determine whether you have a good rapport with the person who will become a key figure in your budgie's life. Here are some questions to discuss with the vet during your introductory visit:

- How many birds do you treat each week?
- What is your experience with budgies?
- What are the costs for your services?
- How often should my budgie receive health check-ups?
- What types of bird surgery do you perform?
- How are emergencies handled when the office is closed?
- Do you make house calls?

The first vet visit

On your budgie's first visit to the veterinarian, the staff will collect important information about your bird's age, sex, weight, and current diet. Before performing a physical examination, the veterinarian might gently restrain your budgie in a towel to prevent injury, and the exam will likely include checking the eyes, ears, nares, mouth, legs, toes, and wings for abnormalities. The vet will also examine the general condition of the feathers and gently feel the crop for signs of impaction. Depending on your bird's health and age, the veterinarian might recommend a routine blood test, and a fecal analysis to check for parasites. All of this information will be recorded to establish your budgie's health baseline, which will serve as a point of reference if your bird develops health issues in the future.

Signs of a sick budgie

Budgies are generally very hardy birds, but even with the best of care they can still get injured or develop an illness. As you become more familiar with your healthy budgie's appearance and behavior, it will be easier for you to recognize signs that he is unwell. Monitor any changes in behavior and physical signs that there might be a problem. Because birds can sometimes be ill for several hours or even days before they display observable symptoms, contact your veterinarian as soon as possible if you think your budgie might be sick or injured.

If your budgie's behavior or appearance suddenly changes, look for the following common signs of illness:

Lethargy: A normally active budgie that doesn't seem interested in playing with toys or interacting with you may be feeling under the weather.

Loss of appetite: Budgies have a high metabolism. Eating less than usual could indicate your bird is sick.

Runny eyes: Contact the veterinarian if you notice a runny discharge from your budgie's eyes, cere, or vent.

Fluffed-up feathers: A healthy budgie will fluff up his feathers from time to time as a way to relax. A budgie that doesn't feel well will remain still and keep his feathers fluffed up for prolonged periods of time.

Sleepiness: Sleeping more than usual can indicate illness, especially if your budgie begins sleeping on two feet when he normally sleeps on one foot, or if he lies down on a perch or crouches on the bottom of the cage.

Labored breathing: Panting, gasping, or wheezing can indicate that your bird has become overheated, has developed a respiratory infection, or has inhaled an airborne irritant. With female budgies, panting can also be a symptom of egg binding.

Tail bobbing: If your bird's tail feathers are bobbing up and down as he rests on a perch, and he isn't short of breath from recent exercise, it might indicate a possible respiratory problem.

Limping: If your budgie has trouble walking, he may have sustained a leg injury, developed a bacterial infection, or been exposed to a toxic substance.

Feather loss: It is normal for budgies to shed their old feathers and grow new ones while they are molting. If your bird begins to lose feathers outside the normal molting process, it could be a sign of stress, nutritional deficiency, or illness, and you should contact the veterinarian.

Wing drooping: Drooping wings are a sign of illness. A single drooping wing may indicate that the wing has been injured.

Unusual droppings: If your bird's diet hasn't changed, watery droppings, or droppings that are yellow, red, or black may indicate a health problem. Consider it an emergency if you see blood in the droppings.

Ask the Experts!

Signs of distress the first few weeks

In the first few weeks after acquiring a budgie, new owners should monitor for atypical behaviors that may indicate health issues. Key signs include the bird being unusually quiet or lethargic, sitting puffed up (a common sign of illness in birds), not eating, or showing labored breathing. These symptoms could be indicators of stress from the new environment or more serious health problems. Regular observation and quick responses to these behaviors are crucial to ensure the well-being of the budgie.

> If your bird is puffed up, sitting at the bottom of the cage, sleeping often, and not eating, these are all signs that there is something wrong. Sometimes your budgie won't eat the first day or so, but that's normal. If it continues, consult an avian vet or the breeder if that's where you got your budgie."

JENNIFER TAYLOR,
Jennifer's budgies

> Atypical behaviors to watch out for in a new bird are excessive puffiness of feathers, lethargy, and a dirty vent. These are the most common things you will see in a budgie that is ill. Budgies, being prey animals, are very good at hiding their illnesses. Other things to look out for are feather breakage and any weird plumage issues. These could be signs of French molt, PBFD, or polyoma. A bird itching excessively could be a sign of mites. Scaly face mites are very noticeable and cause crustiness on the feet and speckled ridged lesions on the beak."

SHANNON COCHRAN,
Chesapeake Aviary

> Most single baby budgies don't move about much when going into a new home. Many are like statues for the first couple of days. Sometimes not eating for the first day is normal. None of this indicates anything wrong other than the transition of going to a new home."

PAUL LEWIS,
Birds Unlimited

> *The most important thing is to ensure that the new budgie is eating. Be aware that seed hulls in the dish should be blown away so the bird can find the seed beneath. Sitting puffed up and hunched over are never good signs. Budgie illnesses are very difficult to diagnose and even more difficult to treat in time."*

SUSAN M. ANDRESEN,

Bull City budgiesr4rfgr

> *Atypical behavior is fluffing up, closed eyes, staying on the bottom of the cage, lack of appetite, tail bobbing, head tucked (although head tucking can be normal if the budgie is merely resting, if they're not feeling well, they will also tuck their heads). Throwing up could be a respiratory issue, something going on with the crop, or possibly they ate something that upset their stomach. A visit to an avian vet is needed."*

DIANE P HYDE,

Long Island Parrot Society

> *Birds are prey in the wild. They have mastered the art of not looking sick. If something is off with your bird, you know the animal best ... Get to the vet fast. Weighing birds regularly is one of the best ways to catch an illness. Most likely the bird will lose weight before he appears to be visually sick. Sick birds should be kept warm, hydrated, and as calm as possible until you can get them to the vet."*

LESLIE CORYN,

Featherbelle Aviary

CHAPTER 5

Bringing Your Budgie Home

Introducing your budgie to his new home

Letting him get to know his cage

The day to bring your budgie home has finally arrived! It's an exciting time for both of you, and a wonderful opportunity to help your bird feel safe and comfortable right from the start. Budgies are naturally sensitive to change, and moving to a new environment can be stressful for them. Before introducing your budgie to his new home, make certain the cage is fully set up with perches, toys, and enough fresh food and water for the first 24 hours. Ideally, fill the food dish with exactly the same pellets or seed he has been accustomed to eating. Don't begin offering fruit, vegetables, or unfamiliar foods until after he has had time to adjust to his new surroundings. Be sure the room where the cage is located is relatively dark at night so your budgie will be able to get enough rest. Birds need about 12 hours of good-quality sleep each night. If necessary, place a dark sheet or towel over the top half of the cage at night to shield the sleeping area from excessive ambient light.

When transferring your budgie from a box or travel carrier to his new cage, try to make the transition as smooth and gentle as possible. If you bring your budgie home in a travel carrier, you might be able to place the carrier next to the cage and allow your bird to leave the carrier on his own without having to physically remove him. To do this safely, open the

door to the cage and place the carrier next to the cage with both doors in alignment. Use a large sheet or towel to block the sides of the carrier and the cage to prevent your budgie from escaping. Then carefully open the carrier door and step aside to wait for your bird to exit the carrier and enter the cage. After he has entered the cage, close the cage door and move the carrier out of the way.

Giving him time to adjust

During the first few days after his arrival, help your budgie relax and become familiar with the sights and sounds of his new environment through graded, gentle handling from day one, allowing for rest time in

between. It's normal for your bird to feel apprehensive and somewhat overwhelmed as he adjusts to his new home. Depending on his personality and previous surroundings, he might sit still in the cage without making a sound for a day or two, and he might avoid eating or drinking when you are around. Engage with your budgie by gently interacting with him, especially if he is hand-raised. Offer your hand slowly and allow him to come to you at his own pace, but avoid making abrupt movements that might startle him. Avoid playing loud music or making loud noises near the cage. Before your budgie can begin to trust you, he will need to feel safe and secure in his cage and comfortable in your presence. Be sure to check on your budgie several times each day, interacting with him gently and allowing him to become accustomed to your touch. When you enter the room or approach the cage, talk to him in a soft, soothing voice and allow him to see your face so he can start getting used to you. If you have already named your budgie, frequently say his name in the same tone of voice, and begin repeating some of the words and phrases you will typically use when you interact with him. Budgies are intelligent, social creatures, and before long they begin to develop a strong bond with the people they recognize and trust.

Letting him get to know you

About a week after bringing your budgie home, gradually increase the amount of time you spend with him each day. Talk or sing to him frequently in a soothing tone to let him get used to the sound of your voice. Talking mimics the budgerigar's natural flock behavior and signals that everything is safe and secure. Say your budgie's name often, but don't expect him to respond by coming closer to you. At this stage, you are just helping him feel more comfortable around you. Place a chair a short distance from the cage where your budgie will be able to see you. Several times a day, slowly walk over to the chair and quietly sit down for 10 to 15 minutes and read a book, or engage in some other peaceful activity. At this early stage of your relationship, try not to stare at your budgie or make eye contact, which could signal to him that you are a predator sizing him up as a potential meal!

Two or three times a day, slowly approach the cage and gently place your hand on the side. Let your hand remain there for a few seconds before slowly moving it away. This will help your budgie realize that your hand is nothing to be afraid of, and it will make it easier for you to begin taming and training him later on. Although progress may seem slow at first, your budgie will soon begin to accept your presence without fluttering or showing other signs of nervousness as you start to develop a relationship of trust with your new companion.

INFO BOX

The 3-3-3 Rule

Leslie Coryn, Featherbelle Aviary

"In dog adoptions, you hear people talking about the 3-3-3 rule. Three days. Three weeks. Three months. In fact, this can be applied to bringing a baby budgie home as well. In the first three days, your budgie will feel a bit overwhelmed. The bird may feel so afraid that it hides under a toy or in the back of the cage quietly. Make sure the budgie has millet available to support it nutritionally and sit by the side of the cage. Talk to your baby in a calm, soft voice. When your bird starts exploring the cage more, it is starting to settle in. This is the time to start handling your bird. Open the door of the cage and see if the budgie comes out on its own. Make sure the room is secured. Now it's time to start teaching your baby to step up. Not all babies understand how to step up. You can use a stick or your finger and have some millet in your hand, and say, 'Step up.' When your baby starts stepping up, be sure to give a treat, smile, and praise your baby. By the third week, you and your bird will be more comfortable and getting used to your home, the sounds, the smells, and your routine. By three months, your bird will feel secure with you. You will be bonding, getting used to each other's quirks. I always make sure doors and windows are closed. I have seen people's birds drown in toilet water, so make sure bathrooms are closed. Make sure the budgie is secure from other animals. Your bird will not become tame with you and get used to you and your hands unless you handle him/her. So even if the bird doesn't feel like it, let it out a few minutes every day and gradually increase the time you are handling your budgie."

Budgies and noise

Noise levels and sounds

Although budgies are considered one of the quietest pet birds, they do make more noise than many other pets. In the Australian outback, budgies primarily communicate with other flock members by making a variety of sounds, whether to raise an alarm, show interest in a prospective mate, or reassure the flock that all is well. In captivity, budgies tend to chatter from dawn to dusk and stop making noise only when it begins to get dark. "It is good to be aware of the noise," says breeder Shannon Cochran of Chesapeake Aviary in Maryland. "While the noise level isn't extremely high, it can be pretty consistent."

Even solitary birds will vocalize regularly by singing, chirping, warbling, and occasionally mimicking familiar words and sounds they hear around the house. Male budgies are more likely to deliver a continual stream of chatter, and they are also more adept at learning to talk. Although female budgies don't usually chatter and warble quite as much as males do, they still generate noise throughout the day and make calls to locate other flock members. After your budgie settles in and adjusts to his new home, you will discover whether he is a relatively quiet bird or more of a chatterbox. Because budgies are small birds, they are not exceptionally

FUN FACT

Social Creatures

In the wild, budgies travel in flocks of as little as three or as many as thousands of birds. These swarms of birds are known to be noisy as they migrate north for winter. Budgies are very social, so it's uncommon to see solitary budgies in the wild.

loud, and most people find the noise levels acceptable, but there are several things that might prompt your budgie to make more noise than usual.

If the cage is kept in a part of the house where you entertain guests, or where there is generally a lot of activity, your budgie's vocalizations might become louder as he attempts to join in the conversation. It is also common for budgies to respond loudly to the songs and calls of wild birds, especially when the cage is adjacent to an outside window. Likewise, if the cage is located near a television set and the volume is often loud, your budgie might instinctively attempt to compete with the ambient noise in the room. Many budgie owners find budgie chatter entertaining and even relaxing. If you think you are likely to be distracted by the noise, or if you simply need a more quiet place to work during the day, consider placing the budgie cage in a bedroom or family room, rather than your home workspace.

Ask the Experts!

Care and Cleaning Schedules

New budgie owners might not be aware of the importance of regular care routines to maintain their bird's health and happiness. Weekly or monthly tasks should include thorough cage cleaning to prevent the buildup of waste and bacteria, checking and replacing toys and perches to ensure they are safe and stimulating, and monitoring the bird's health, including its nails and beak, for any signs of overgrowth or illness. These routines are vital for creating a safe and enriching environment for the budgie.

Cleaning the cage is a good weekly habit that is made easier if you place several layers of paper on the bottom at a time. This way you can just remove the top one and throw it away. Water should be changed daily, and the cup should be thoroughly washed weekly."

SUSAN M. ANDRESEN,

Bull City budgies

"Some people choose to clean their cage daily/every other day/weekly. It really depends on how dirty the cage gets. Fresh water should be given daily. I like to try and change up the toys every month or so to keep them interested."

JENNIFER TAYLOR,
Jennifer's Budgies

"Toy/equipment checks are an important thing that many people overlook with birds. Budgies, being very active, can quickly get themselves into trouble. Keeping a regular schedule for monitoring the condition of their toys, perches, cages, etc., can save you a lot of heartbreak. Loose strings on rope perches or toys can easily entrap a budgie."

SHANNON COCHRAN,
Chesapeake Aviary

"You'll want to clean the cage at least weekly, and I strongly recommend using a cage grate so that waste and soft foods go through the grate and are then unable to be picked up by the birds. The grate will likely end up with waste stuck to it though, so it's important to keep it clean. Please do NOT place paper on top of the grate to save yourself the cleaning aspect, as this totally defeats the purpose of the grate!"

ANITA GOLDEN,
formerly Nita's Nest

"Cages need to be cleaned daily (and food and water must be changed daily); however, on a weekly basis, all toys need to be inspected to make sure there are no loose threads/parts where the budgies can get their nails caught. Run the food/water dishes through the dishwasher once a week. Make sure there is no food accumulation in the corner of the cages that could promote bacteria."

DIANE P HYDE,
Long Island Parrot Society

Wing clipping

What is wing clipping?

Wing clipping is the practice of selectively trimming some of the primary flight feathers on the wing in order to limit a bird's ability to fly. When these feathers are trimmed correctly, a budgie will not be able to fly as high or as fast as he normally would, but he will still be able to fly a couple of feet into the air and flutter back down and land safely on the ground. The procedure is painless and roughly equivalent to getting a haircut. There are several styles of wing clipping, but usually just the first five to seven of the 10 primary flight feathers are trimmed off about halfway between the base and the tip of the feather, and the secondary flight feathers are not trimmed. The feathers are clipped evenly on both wings to enable the bird to control his descent when landing. All of the trimmed feathers will eventually grow back to their usual length, and the budgie will be able to fly normally again.

But feathers don't grow continuously like human hair. They fall out and are replaced with new feathers during a budgie's natural molt cycle, which usually occurs about once or twice a year. So, if a budgie's wings are to remain clipped for a period of time, the flight feathers must be checked

Photo Courtesy of David Morgan

regularly to see if new feathers have replaced any of the trimmed feathers, in which case the new feathers will also need to be trimmed. Strictly speaking, a healthy budgie doesn't need to have his wings clipped. However, under certain conditions, wing clipping might be appropriate to help prevent a budgie from escaping, or to reduce the chance of exposure to dangerous situations around the home, and a veterinarian might prescribe wing clipping to help a bird recover from an injury.

Why would wings be clipped?

Although it is a common practice, wing clipping is a controversial subject. Some bird enthusiasts and veterinarians recommend it, while others oppose it. Safety is the primary reason that many budgie owners choose to clip their bird's wings. When a budgie's wings are clipped, he is less likely to fly out an open door or window, and if he does manage to escape there is a better chance of recovering him. This does not mean it is safe to take your budgie outside after his wings have been trimmed. Although he may not be able to fly very far under his own power, he could easily soar into the sky if a stiff breeze carries him away. A budgie may also face a number of potential dangers inside the home when he is allowed to fly outside the cage, including ceiling fans, closed windows, mirrors, hot stoves, sinks, and toilets. Flying into any one of these hazards could result in serious injury or death, and wing clipping reduces a bird's exposure to these perils. Wing clipping is also sometimes used to facilitate taming and training. A budgie with trimmed wings is more dependent and easier to tame than one that can fly around the room, and after a bird has learned a few basic commands, wing clipping can be discontinued.

Others contend that wing clipping often creates more problems than it solves. In captivity, budgies can become overweight if they do not get enough exercise, and flying is the most natural way for a bird to exercise. Wing clipping can also make some budgies more prone to behavioral issues such as feather plucking. Although wing clipping can prevent a bird from flying into hazardous situations, it also prevents a bird from using flight as a means of escape, which can render a budgie more vulnerable to attack if there are other pets in the house that might view a small, flightless bird as a quick meal. Though it may require a little more patience, taming and training a

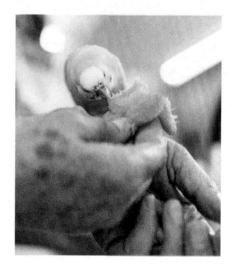

budgie can be accomplished without clipping the wings, and many assert that budgies are happier and more likely to form a close bond with the owner when their wings are not clipped. Ultimately, wing clipping is a personal decision, and you should carefully weigh the potential advantages and disadvantages before determining what is best for your bird's health and safety.

If you choose to clip your budgie's wings

Many budgie owners find it more convenient to simply let a professional clip their bird's wings. Before you attempt to clip your budgie's wings yourself, ask someone who is experienced in wing clipping to guide you through the procedure, such as an avian veterinarian, a budgie breeder, or the owner of a pet shop that sells birds. You could seriously injure your bird if you attempt to clip his wings without first receiving guided instruction.

Choose an appropriate location to clip your bird's wings. The room should be well-lighted, so you can clearly see what you are doing; and if

the room has doors or windows, you must be able to securely close them to prevent escape in the event your bird gets loose during the procedure. It's also better to have an assistant hold your budgie, so that both of your hands are free to gently spread the wings and clip the feathers. Make sure you have all the supplies you may need on hand before you begin. You will need a sharp pair of scissors to trim the feathers, cornstarch and needle-nose pliers in case you accidentally clip a blood feather, and possibly a small towel to restrain your bird.

If an assistant will be holding your budgie, have the person gently grasp your budgie in one hand, cradling the bird's back against the inside of the palm and gently curling the fingers around the bird's lower body without putting pressure on the bird's chest. The assistant can then use the thumb and forefinger of the other hand to gently but firmly hold the bird's head to prevent biting. Gently spread one wing to identify the primary flight feathers on the lower part of the wing, and the shorter feathers, called coverts, that overlap the upper part of the flight feathers. You will be trimming the first five to seven of the primary flight feathers, without cutting any of the shorter coverts that overlap them. Carefully examine each feather before clipping it to make certain you do not cut any blood feathers. These are new feathers that still have a dark shaft and a visible blood vessel running through them. If a blood feather is cut, it will bleed profusely and will need to be removed with pliers. After removing the feather, cornstarch must be applied to the area to stop the bleeding.

Beginning at the tip of the wing, clip the first primary feather about one-quarter inch below the overlapping covert feathers. Clip one feather at a time, and try to make a clean cut across the feather shaft because ragged feathers may cause irritation and lead to feather plucking.

CELEBRITY BUDGIES
Hollywood Birds

Budgies have been a popular Hollywood pet through the ages. American actor and film director Clint Eastwood loved budgies and has even been photographed with his pet birds. Actress Marilyn Monroe also owned two budgies, Bobo and Clyde. And more recently, pop icon Britney Spears brought budgies into her life in 2007 and 2009. Spears initially went to the pet store for dog food but reportedly couldn't leave without a pair of budgies.

Move on to the next primary feather, and continue trimming each of the feathers about one-quarter inch below the overlapping covert feathers. When you have finished trimming the fifth feather, trim the feathers on the other wing. Clip an equal number of feathers on each wing to allow your budgie to maintain his equilibrium. After trimming the second wing, take your budgie to a safe, enclosed room for a test flight. He should be able to fly several feet above the floor and gently flutter back down. If your budgie can still fly almost as high as the ceiling, you will also need to clip the sixth and seventh primary feathers on both wings.

INFO BOX

Weekly Safety Checklist

Misty Maruska & Melody Maruska, Parrots N Stuff

There is no such thing as a toy, cage, perch, or any other item that is 100% bird-safe. It is important to regularly check everything to avoid potential hazards. Here is a basic checklist to help keep your feathered friends safe!

- *Look at all toys and perches with rope or string: If there are long pieces, frayed, or knotted pieces, trim them down to avoid your bird getting stuck.*

- *Check your bird's nails and beak: Are these curving to where they are getting caught on carpet, clothing, or toys and perches? If yes, it is probably time to trim. Temporarily take out the item to avoid injury.*

INFO BOX

Weekly Safety Checklist

- *Check all wire or plastic chain: Has the bird pried them open to where it can hook its feet or beak in them? If yes, remove the item completely.*

- *Check all plastic and hard toys: Has your bird chewed them to where there are sharp pieces or cracks the budgie could get stuck in, etc.? If so, remove them.*

- *Inspect the cage itself: Has the bird broken the welding or chewed through something it could get stuck in, sneak out of the cage, or cut itself on? If so, a new cage or repairs are needed.*

- *Are all toy clips, clamps, or other hardware securely fastened?*

- *Are all parts of the cage where they should be—the tray pushed all the way in, doors latched correctly, etc.?*

CHAPTER 6

Training Your Budgie

Handling

Taming

After your budgie has settled into his new surroundings, and he is comfortable with your presence near the cage, you can begin taming him. The taming process can take anywhere from a few days to several weeks, depending on your bird's personality and his previous experience

with human interaction. The key to taming your budgie is patience, so don't try to rush the process. The goal is to encourage your bird to trust you, which will pave the way to successful training later on. Be sure to continue topping off his food and water dishes every day so he will begin to recognize that you are the one giving him food. This will help you gain his trust, and he will be excited to see you when you enter the room.

By now your budgie should remain calm when you slowly approach and gently place your hand on the side of the cage and leave it there for a few seconds before moving it away. The next step is to teach him that your hand is not a threat, even when it is inside the cage. Place a chair next to the cage so you can sit down, open the cage door, and put your hand in the cage. Several times a day, talk to your budgie in a soothing voice as you approach the cage and sit down in the chair. Continue talking as you slowly open the cage door and put your hand inside. Try to keep your hand below your bird when you place it in the cage because budgies are naturally wary of predators swooping down from above to attack. Let your hand remain in the cage for several minutes as you continue talking to your bird, and avoid making sudden movements that might startle him. Try to repeat these taming sessions three or four times a day, allowing at least half an hour to pass before the next session. If your budgie seems threatened by your hand, you might need to do this for several days until he gradually becomes accustomed to your hand being inside his cage.

Small steps before training

Some budgie owners enjoy training their budgies to perform elaborate tricks, while others just want their birds to feel comfortable and unafraid when interacting with other family members. Whichever side of the training spectrum you fall on, there are four basic skills every budgie should learn that will make it easier to handle him safely and allow him to become the great pet he has the potential to be. Keep training sessions short, about 10 or 15 minutes long, and repeat them several times throughout the day.

Hand training

Once your budgie feels safe with your hand inside the cage, you can start preparing him to accept physical contact with your hand and fingers. The best way to do this is to bribe your budgie with a favorite treat, such as millet spray. Millet sprays are long stalks of millet seed, and most budgies can't resist them. You can use millet spray to your best advantage by offering it only when you are taming and training your budgie. Place your hand inside the cage while holding a small piece of millet spray between your thumb and index finger, and slowly move your hand toward your budgie to offer him the treat. Your bird may back away from your hand at first, but eventually he won't be able to resist the millet.

Tempt your budgie to eat millet spray from your hand three or four times a day, and talk to him as you do this to help him associate your hand and fingers with your soothing voice and a delicious treat. When your budgie is comfortable eating out of your hand, try placing the back of your finger against his chest to see if he will accept physical contact without moving away. Once he allows you to touch him, try gently stroking his breast with the back of your finger. This will prepare him to learn the "finger perch" behavior.

As you begin to have more physical contact with your budgie, remember to always be as gentle as possible when handling your bird. Don't squeeze him or grasp him too firmly. Never attempt to grab him by the wings, legs, or tail. This will frighten him, and could potentially break delicate bones or damage internal organs. To safely hold your budgie, cradle your bird in one hand with his back against the inside of your palm. Gently fold your thumb, ring finger, and little finger around your bird's lower body without putting pressure on the bird's chest, and support his neck by placing your index and middle fingers on either side of the head.

Finger perch

Now that your budgie has become accustomed to having your hand inside the cage, and will allow you to gently touch him, you can begin training him to perch on your finger. Teaching your bird this command will make it much easier to take him out of the cage and return him again.

You can also use this command when you want to inspect your budgie for signs of illness or injury. To teach your bird this command, reach into the cage and place your outstretched finger just below the perch he is resting on. Slowly move your finger above the perch and gently rub the top of his legs, while saying "step up" in an encouraging tone of voice. If your budgie seems reluctant to step onto your finger when you give the "step up" command, try using your other hand to hold a piece of spray millet in a place where he will be forced to step onto your finger in order to reach the treat.

Praise your bird and offer him a treat when he steps onto your finger and practice the training sessions several times a day. Within a few days, your budgie should hop onto your finger whenever you give the command. Once your budgie is comfortable with using your finger as a perch, try slowly moving him around inside the cage while he is perched on your finger. Your budgie may jump off when you do this, but keep practicing until he thinks of your finger as a secure place to perch.

Step up

In addition to teaching your budgie to perch on your finger, the "step-up" command is also very useful for transferring your budgie from your finger to a perch inside the cage, or for retrieving your bird from a high shelf or light fixture in a room. Start by putting your hand in the cage next to the perch your budgie is sitting on, and then say "step up" to ask your budgie to step onto your finger. Take your bird out of the cage, and then offer the index finger of the other hand as a perch and say "step up" again. When your budgie moves from one finger to the other, praise him and offer him a treat when he successfully transfers to the other finger. Repeat this a few times to reinforce the concept that "step up" means to step onto a new perch that is being offered.

Some trainers prefer to use a different phrase, such as "step down," when they want a budgie to transfer to a lower perch, and "step up" to ask a budgie to transfer to a higher perch. Either method is successful when these commands are used consistently. After training your budgie to transfer from one finger to another when you say "step up," increase the distance between your fingers before you give the command so your bird has to fly a short distance from one finger to the other. Once he has mastered this, try using the step-up command to ask your bird to fly over and land on your raised finger from wherever he is perched outside the cage.

Towel training

Towel training teaches your budgie to feel relaxed and comfortable while being wrapped in a soft, smooth towel. This can be very helpful when it is necessary to safely restrain your bird if he is sick or injured or to hold him securely when he is having his wings clipped or his nails trimmed. Begin by laying the towel flat on a table and placing one of your budgie's favorite treats or toys in the center of the towel. Let your budgie walk around and explore the towel while you speak to him and interact with him for a few minutes. Practice these sessions a number of times until your bird is comfortable exploring the towel when it is lying flat on the table.

The next step is to slowly pull one corner of the towel up and over him while you gently speak to him and pet him. When your budgie is used to having one corner of the towel pulled over him, move on to a second corner, and then a third, until you can loosely close the towel around him. Repeat these wrapping sessions every day and provide plenty of treats. Eventually your budgie will learn to accept being covered.

Speaking

General noises

As you spend time with your budgie, you will begin to distinguish the many different vocalizations he makes and will be able to discern what the bird is attempting to communicate. Here are some of the more common sounds that budgies make and what they might mean.

Contented Chatter: Throughout the day, budgies will chirp, warble, and occasionally make clicking noises to reassure their flock members that they are happy and everything is all right.

Singing: Budgies don't sing in the same way that songbirds warble a melody. But they will often use a variety of chirps, tweets, whistles, and other sounds they have learned to sing along with when they hear music they like.

Contact Call: If your budgie misses you, or thinks you might be lost, he might make a long, sustained call, which can be described as a long chirp, tweet, or whistle. You can let your budgie know that you are not lost by answering with your own call in a reassuring tone.

Distress Call: The distress call is louder and more insistent than the contact call, and it means that your budgie is alarmed by something and making you aware of a problem. The source of the trouble might be an issue with something in the cage—perhaps a perch has fallen down, or a food or water dish needs to be refilled. It could mean that the budgie has seen something frightening, such as a cat or a hawk outside the window. A distress call could also mean that your budgie has injured himself in some way, so it is important to check on him when you hear this call to make sure he is safe. Once you have determined that all is well, if your budgie continues to squawk, you can try to restore calm by talking to him in a gentle voice.

Teaching your budgie to speak

Budgies are quite vocal, and many of them can mimic the sound of the human voice as well as larger parrots. Teaching a budgie to speak is a relatively simple process, but it does require dedication, patience, and plenty of repetition. It's best to start teaching your budgie to talk as soon as you bring him home, as they are more impressionable when they are younger, and you don't want to waste any of those early weeks. Single words of one or two syllables are often easier for a budgie to learn, and teaching your bird his own name is a good way to begin. After your bird has learned a few individual words, you can try teaching him some short phrases.

Associating words and phrases with specific actions can also make it easier for budgies to learn how to speak. For example, you can say "good bird" when he responds correctly to a command, or "Would you like treat?" when you offer him a favorite snack. Choose a relatively quiet room for speech training, so that your budgie isn't distracted by the television, radio, or other human voices. To help your budgie remain interested in learning to speak, repeat the training sessions two or three times a day, for no more than 10 or 15 minutes at a time. Some budgies seem to respond better to voices in a higher register, so if you have

a lower voice, try to use a higher range when teaching your budgie to speak, and always say the words clearly and enthusiastically. When your budgie is first learning to mimic human speech, his words may sound garbled, but it is important for you to recognize his efforts to learn the language of his new "flock." Be sure to praise your bird and repeat the words back to him. This will encourage your bird to continue learning new words and phrases.

Keys to training

Training your budgie can be great fun for both you and your new companion, but it will require time and patience. All budgies have their own personalities, and the amount of time it takes to teach a bird a particular behavior will vary. Some budgies may learn a new trick after just a few short training sessions, while others may require several weeks of training. Choose a training area with few distractions so your budgie will be able to focus his attention on his interaction with you. For best results, limit the training sessions to no more than 15 minutes, and repeat them two or three times a day. Try to end each session on a positive note so your budgie is encouraged to continue learning and will be excited to begin the next session. Consistency is also very important. Always use the same command when teaching your bird a new trick to help him understand what you want him to do. Start with simple tricks before moving on to more complicated behaviors. Above all, remember to reward your bird with treats and praise when he successfully completes a task.

Tricks

Climb the ladder

Budgies love to climb, so this trick is easy for most of them to learn. Begin by setting up a toy ladder that is designed for budgies outside the cage. With your budgie out of the cage and perched on your finger, use the "step-up" command to ask him to leave your finger and step onto the first rung of the ladder. Hold your budgie's favorite treat at the top of the ladder, and say the word or phrase you have chosen for this trick to encourage him to climb all the way to the top of the ladder. Reward your bird with praise and a treat when he reaches the top.

Practice this several times until you can give the command to climb the ladder, without holding a treat at the top, and your bird will successfully climb the ladder. Now place your bird a short distance away from the ladder and repeat your "climb the ladder" command to encourage him to walk over and climb up the ladder. Be sure to reward your budgie with praise and a treat when he climbs to the top. When your budgie has mastered this concept, you can gradually place your bird farther and farther away from the ladder and he will walk or fly to the ladder and climb up when you give the command.

FUN FACT
Super Ears

Fetch

Budgies enjoy playing fetch, and it's a great way to bond with your bird. Begin by choosing a suitable toy or some other object that your bird can carry in his beak. The object must be small enough for your bird to pick up and carry, but not so small that it could become a choking

Despite having no visible ears (budgies' ears are internal and hidden by plumage), these remarkable little birds have excellent hearing. Budgies have a hearing range of 400–20,000 Hz and are often capable of mimicking sounds. Like other parrots, budgies can be trained to repeat words, phrases, and songs. Experts suggest that male budgies often learn to speak more quickly, but females can also learn to talk and whistle tunes.

hazard. A small lattice ball or a brightly colored plastic ring are good choices for this trick. Once you have selected an appropriate toy, place it in your budgie's cage and allow him to become familiar with it for a day or two. You can encourage him to show interest in the toy by occasionally making it move. After your budgie has become comfortable around the toy, take him out of the cage and set him on a flat surface such as a table. Put the toy in front of your bird and say "fetch." When he picks it up, praise him and offer a treat so that he understands that this trick involves picking up the toy. Repeat the process several times to teach your budgie to consistently pick up the toy when you say "fetch." The next step is to start placing your hand in front of your bird after he picks up the toy, so it will fall into your hand when he drops it. When your budgie drops the toy into your hand, praise him and offer a treat so he will associate dropping the toy in your hand with receiving the reward. Repeat this process for several days. After your budgie has learned to consistently pick up the toy and drop it into your hand when you say "fetch," you can gradually increase the distance you throw the toy, and your bird will scurry over to pick it up and drop it in your hand.

Ask the Experts!

Training Advice

Training budgies requires patience, consistent effort, and a tailored approach to each bird's interests and capabilities. Positive reinforcement through treats like millet can motivate budgies to learn tricks and words. Speaking training benefits from repetitive and clear articulation in a quiet, distraction-free environment. Males are generally more apt at speaking, with frequent, short sessions being most effective for teaching new words or phrases.

" *Use millet as a positive reinforcer when training. Since most budgies enjoy millet, only use it for training—you'll get better results."*

DIANE P HYDE,

Long Island Parrot Society

" *First your budgie will need to be tamed and comfortable with you. Watch what the bird is interested in playing with and see if it can be structured into a 'trick' like dropping paper clips off the side of a table. For learning to speak, take the bird into a small, dimly lit room and hold the budgie facing you on your finger. Repeat the same word over and over and over. Many birds learn to talk naturally by hearing the same words repeated many times a day in context."*

SUSAN M. ANDRESEN,

Bull City Budgies

" *Millet (or the bird's favorite food) is a great training aid. Both males and females have the ability to talk ... Females have a vocabulary of up to 100 words; males, over 150. When trying to teach your budgie to talk, repetition is the key. Take time to have speaking lessons with your budgie (15 minutes a couple times a day) and take every opportunity to say the words to your budgie. Before long, he will hopefully be talking."*

JENNIFER TAYLOR,

Jennifer's Budgies

66 *TV programs meant for small children are a great way to teach your budgie to speak. Those shows tend to enunciate words more clearly and speak a lot slower. This can help your budgie learn. Repeating words to the bird when it is engaged with you and being rewarded will also help. It is important to understand that birds hilariously tend to pick up and learn words you aren't expecting them to."*

SHANNON COCHRAN,

Chesapeake Aviary

66 *I once read that birds have a much easier time saying words that contain the letter R. For this reason, 'pretty bird' seems to be the easiest phrase for a bird to learn. I once had a single cockatiel that learned 'pretty bird' and then taught the rest of the bird room simply saying it over and over when I wasn't there! Once a bird learns the first phrase, it seems it is easier for them to learn more. Both male and female budgies can speak, though not every budgie will learn to speak and males are more likely to learn."*

ANITA GOLDEN,

formerly Nita's Nest

CHAPTER 7

Breeding Budgies

Breeding basics

Breeding season

Many wild birds are seasonal breeders that mate and build nests during certain times of the year. Budgies are opportunistic breeders that breed whenever environmental conditions are favorable for raising their offspring. In Australia, wild budgies usually reproduce after rainfall,

when grass seed is plentiful and freshwater lakes and ponds provide a reliable source of drinking water. Because budgies in captivity have a consistent supply of food and water year-round, they may breed at any time of year. Budgies can, however, be fussy about choosing mates and nesting sites, and they may refuse to breed if they are apprehensive about something in their surroundings.

If you have a male and female budgie, but you do not want them to breed, there are several things you can do to discourage breeding. Make sure there is nothing in the cage that your birds might use as a nesting site, such as a nest box, a bird hut, or a bowl on the bottom of the cage. Budgie hens are minimalists when it comes to choosing a nesting site, and anything that resembles a cozy place to hide or lay eggs can stimulate the hen's breeding instinct. Also, limit the amount of high-calorie and fatty foods

HELPFUL TIP
Mates for Life

Budgies are monogamous birds and typically remain with their partner while raising their chicks. In some cases, budgies will form lasting bonds with their mate and reject any bird that comes between them. Signs of budgie bonding can include grooming each other, sharing a perch, and touching beaks. Mating signs in budgies can consist of a male budgie sharing or providing food and a female lifting her tail feathers and wings. Non-bonded budgie pairs may remain monogamous while their chicks are young but move on to a new partner once the chicks have flown the nest.

you feed your birds to help reduce the inclination to breed. In addition, you can rearrange the location of the toys, ladders, perches, and food and water dishes in the cage. Budgies prefer to breed in a stable environment and routinely altering their surroundings can help discourage breeding. If taking steps to discourage your budgies from breeding is unsuccessful, you might need to keep the birds in separate cages.

Sooner or later, most budgie owners think about breeding their birds. Here are some things to consider before you decide to encourage your budgies to produce offspring:

- Are the birds you intend to breed in excellent health?
- Will an avian veterinarian be available if there is an emergency?
- Are you prepared for the expense of additional equipment, food, and veterinary visits?
- Can you hand-feed the young birds if the parents reject them?
- Will you be able to keep the offspring if you cannot find good homes for them?

Setting up for breeding

A breeding pair of budgies will need a large cage about 24 inches long, 16 inches wide, and 16 inches tall. Set up the cage with several wood perches, food and water dishes, and a few toys. Because budgies do not build twig nests as some birds do, you must provide the pair with a nest box that mimics the tree hollows that wild budgies often use as a nesting site.

Budgie nest boxes are available at pet stores and online, and there are two basic styles: vertical and horizontal. Vertical nest boxes are about 10 inches high, 6 inches wide, and 6 inches deep. Horizontal nest boxes are about 10 inches long, 6 inches high, and 6 inches deep. Regardless of which style you choose, the nest box should have a hinged lid that will allow you to check on the hen and chicks if you suspect a problem and a round entrance hole about 1 1/2 to 2 inches in diameter, with a perch below the entrance. The floor of the nest box should have a circular depression about 5 inches in diameter and be three-quarters of an inch deep so the hen can lay her eggs. Attach the nest box to the outside of the cage with the entrance hole facing the inside of the cage. This may require removing a secondary cage door or cutting some of the wire bars on the side of the cage so the birds can access the nest box through the entrance hole.

After installing the nest box, open the lid and place a small handful of soft pine shavings on the bottom, which will serve as a substitute for the wood shavings that a wild budgie hen will produce when she uses her beaks to shape the inside of a hollow tree. The pine shavings will help prevent the chicks from developing a condition called splayed legs, which can occur if the floor of the nest box is too slippery. The hen will arrange the shavings to her liking.

Photo Courtesy of David Morgan

Choosing the pair

The ideal breeding age for male and female budgies is between one and four years old. Although budgies are physically able to breed when they are around six months old, they should not be bred before they are a year old, and some breeders recommend waiting until the birds are two years old. Younger birds are still growing and developing, and breeding them before they are fully mature can physically strain their bodies and lead to health problems. Budgies over four years old are generally considered too old for breeding purposes. If you aren't sure how old your budgies are, an avian vet can evaluate them to determine their approximate ages. You should also make sure that the prospective pair is not closely related. Breeding budgies that are close relatives can increase the risk of genetic disorders and physical defects in the offspring. To avoid such problems, purchase the male and female from two different breeders or from two pet stores that obtain their birds from different sources.

If you purchase a new male or female budgie for breeding purposes, the new bird should be examined by an avian veterinarian and then kept in a separate cage away from other birds for a four-week period of quarantine before being introduced to other birds. When budgies do not know each other, they may fight if they are immediately placed in the same cage, so keep the prospective pair in separate cages and gradually introduce them. Place the cages a few inches apart in the same room so the two birds can get used to each other without becoming territorial and let them out of their cages to play at different times.

After your budgies have spent a week or two getting acquainted with each other, take them out of their cages into a secure room and monitor them as they interact in neutral territory. Expect the two birds to quarrel as they establish a pecking order, but if a minor squabble starts to get out of hand, return the birds to their cages and try introducing them another time. Give the birds several opportunities to interact with each other in neutral territory, and when they are getting along with each other, you can put them together in the breeding cage. If one of the birds has already been living in the cage, clean the cage and rearrange the perches and toys to help make it seem like a more neutral space, and place food and water dishes on opposite sides of the cage so the birds can feed separately if they want to. After putting the birds in the same cage, monitor them for several days to make sure they continue to get along without fighting.

Because your budgies will devote much of their physical energy to laying eggs, incubating the eggs, and feeding the chicks, both birds must be in excellent health before you breed them. If they haven't had a recent veterinary health check-up, take them to an avian veterinarian to verify that they are robust enough to breed without putting their health, or the health of their offspring, at risk. If both birds are healthy, you can begin conditioning them for breeding. Continue to feed them a balanced, nutritious diet, and keep a cuttlebone or mineral block in the cage to supply the calcium and minerals necessary for egg development and eggshell formation. Supplement the diet with egg food to provide the additional protein that budgies need when breeding. Egg food supplement for budgies is available from pet stores and online.

Putting a male and female budgie together in the same cage does not guarantee that they will become a breeding pair. Budgies are monogamous, and the birds must bond with each other before they will mate. If the two birds you intend to breed are already kept in the same cage and get along well with each other, they are likely to bond. In some cases, however, a particular male and female budgie may never bond with each other, and you will have to try a different pairing.

A pair's courtship behavior will usually indicate whether two budgies have bonded with each other. When first introduced, the female will often ignore the male. The male will then try to court the female by sitting next to her on the perch and chirping, bobbing his head up and down, and tapping his beak against her beak. As the courtship progresses, the pair will groom each other, and the male will attempt to feed the female regurgitated food. If the courtship is successful and the birds bond with each other, they will usually mate within a day or two. The female will lift her tail in the air, and the male will stand on top of her and then move sideways and stretch out one wing to hold the female in position as they rub their cloacas together.

Hatchlings and care

Egg laying

After mating, the budgie hen will briefly inspect the nest box. If it meets with her approval, she will begin spending more time inside the box as she prepares to lay eggs and incubate them. The hen will rearrange the wood shavings on the floor of the nest box, and she may toss some of them out if she determines there are too many. Before she lays the first egg, you may notice the hen's abdomen beginning to swell or that her droppings have become larger and less frequent as her body adjusts to accommodate the eggs she is carrying. The hen may also develop an area of bare skin around her vent called a "brood patch," which will help her keep the eggs warm during incubation.

About eight to ten days after mating, the hen will lay the first egg. She will continue to lay an egg every other day until she has a clutch of four to eight eggs. After the second or third egg has been laid, the hen will start sitting on the eggs to incubate them. She will also turn the eggs and change their position in the nest from time to time to make sure they are kept equally warm.

During the incubation period, the hen will spend most of the day and night inside the nest box, occasionally leaving to deposit droppings. The cock will perch outside the entrance at regular intervals to feed the hen regurgitated food. Budgie hens do not like to be disturbed while they are incubating eggs, so try to avoid unnecessary noise and activity in the room that houses the breeding cage. Also, resist the temptation to raise the lid of the nest box more than once or twice a day to check on the eggs and chicks. When you do, check them very quickly when the hen is off the nest.

Fertile budgie eggs can remain viable for up to seven days after they are laid if they are stored at a temperature of about 55 to 60 degrees Fahrenheit and 60% humidity. The eggs can be hatched using an incubator set to a temperature of between 98 and 99 degrees Fahrenheit and 65% humidity. If the incubator does not have an automatic turning feature, you will need to gently turn the eggs 180 degrees from side to side about four to eight times during the day, or about once every hour.

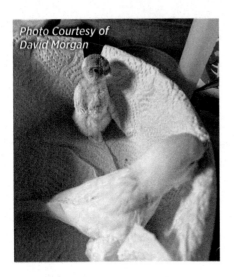

Photo Courtesy of
David Morgan

It is also important to alternate the direction you rotate the eggs each time you turn them. For example, if you turn the eggs clockwise the first time, you should turn the eggs counterclockwise the next time, and so on. This prevents the chalazae, the two thin strands of tissue that hold the yolk in the center of the egg, from twisting and rupturing the yolk sac or the blood vessels in the developing embryo.

Caring for hatchlings

The first egg will usually hatch around 18 days after the hen begins incubating the clutch. The rest of the eggs will hatch about one every other day, in the order they were laid. Because the chicks hatch on different days, some will be older and discernibly larger and more developed than others. Budgie chicks are blind and naked when they hatch, and too weak to raise their heads. They are totally dependent on the mother bird to feed them and keep them warm. Despite their awkward appearance, budgie chicks grow up very quickly.

NOTE:

It is correct that the hen might not start incubating until there are two or three eggs, and in that case, up to three chicks could hatch at once, or on successive days at first. But then the spacing of the rest of the clutch will be every other day. It all depends on when she starts incubating. If she incubates from the first egg, then each chick will hatch two days after the prior one.

Diana Wilkewitz,
Budgiedin Budgerigars

The cock will continue to feed the hen as she cares for the hatchlings, and the hen will feed them every one to two hours for the first few days. As the chicks grow older, the hen will feed them only during the day. Their eyes will open around the seventh day, and by the eleventh day, the chicks will be covered in fluffy down.

About four to five weeks after hatching, the young birds will enter their fledgling stage. They'll begin to develop their flight feathers, and their muscles will be developed enough to allow them to walk around the nest box and exercise their wings. The parents will continue to feed them for another week or so, but as the fledglings become more independent, they will start venturing out of the nest box to explore their surroundings. When they begin leaving the nest, place a flat food dish and a shallow water bowl on the bottom of the cage to encourage the youngsters to start eating and drinking on their own. Offer them soft foods, fresh fruit, vegetables, mixed seeds, and pellets to get them used to the foods they will eat as adults.

Weaning

The weaning process is a critical stage in the young budgies' lives. Within a relatively short time, they will transition from eating the regurgitated food their parents feed them to learning how to eat a variety of foods on their own. Young budgies usually wean from their parents at about five to six weeks of age, but it is important to wait until they have learned how to feed themselves and are eating enough food before separating them from their parents. Monitor the youngsters carefully to make sure they can eat seeds, pellets, fruits, and vegetables and that they can drink water on their own. When they are successfully feeding themselves and no longer depend on their parents to help feed them, they should be moved to another cage. Budgie parents instinctively drive away their offspring when they are weaned, and they will become aggressive toward the young birds if they remain in the same cage.

> 66
>
> *The parents will usually start a second clutch around the time the first clutch is ready to leave the nest, and sometimes before that. Be prepared to move the chicks out quickly at the first sign that either parent is starting to attack them. Not all parents will attack the chicks, but the potential is there and chicks can be maimed or killed. Even the defending parent could be seriously injured. So this is something that needs to be watched out for.*
>
> DIANA WILKEWITZ,
> *Budgiedin Budgerigars*
>
> 99

Set up a cage with food and water dishes, toys, and several perches. Include a low perch at the bottom of the cage to help the fledglings practice perching and climbing. After moving the weaned chicks to this new cage, relocate the hen to a completely different cage, preferably out of sight and hearing of the breeding cage that houses the male and the chicks. This separation helps prevent her from breeding and laying eggs again too soon. With no nest box and no mate, the father will likely do well at weaning the chicks over a longer period of time. Even if the mother cannot be moved entirely out of sight and earshot, separating her to another cage across the room is better than leaving her in the breeding cage. This arrangement allows the father to focus on caring for the chicks while giving the hen a much-needed rest.

Selling hatchlings

Breeding and selling

Budgies have been bred in captivity since the 1850s, and they continue to be one of the most popular pets in the world. Whether you are thinking about breeding and selling budgies as a business or wondering how to sell a few hatchlings, it is useful to know something about the market for these birds. The age and welfare of your hatchlings will be a primary concern for you and for potential buyers. Until they are fully weaned and are about eight to ten weeks old, young budgies are not mature enough to be sold or placed in a new home. Complying with current governmental regulations is also critical. Businesses that involve animals are subject to various legal requirements. To avoid legal complications, check with city, state, and federal agencies to determine if you are required to obtain any permits, licenses, or inspections in order to sell your birds.

HELPFUL TIP

Is It a Boy or a Girl?

It can be challenging to determine the biological sex of a budgie, but one clue lies in the bird's "cere." The cere is a pale patch of waxy skin above the bird's beak. Male budgies generally have a blue cere, while females have a white or reddish-brown cere. In addition, adolescent budgies often have ceres that are reddish white.

Depending on where you live, there may be several potential markets to consider, including local pet stores, online marketplaces, bird shows, and local bird clubs. If you intend to breed and sell budgies as a business, selling your birds locally can also help you establish a reputation as a breeder and get acquainted with buyers and other breeders in your area. Attending bird shows is another way to connect with breeders and prospective buyers who may be able to help you identify additional markets and strategies for your area. Sometimes, letting your friends and acquaintances know that you have budgies for sale can be the most effective marketing strategy of all. Pricing your budgies appropriately can help you attract buyers.

In addition to your breeding costs and the quality of your budgies, consider the demand for similar budgies in your area. Be aware that local pet stores typically buy budgies for much less than they sell them. Bird shows and online marketplaces can often help you sell birds for higher prices.

CHAPTER 8

Living Longer

A healthy budgie

Healthy signs

Although statistics show that the average life span of a budgie in captivity is five to eight years, with proper care, a budgie in good health can live for well over 10 years. According to Guinness World Records, a budgie named Charlie in London, England, lived to be 29 years old!

What can you do to help your budgie live a long and happy life? Monitoring your budgie's health and scheduling regular check-ups with an avian veterinarian can often add many years to his life. Like many wild birds, budgies instinctively hide symptoms of illness to avoid attracting the attention of predators. Knowing what a healthy budgie looks like can help

you determine when your bird is sick and needs veterinary attention before an illness becomes severe. Here are some common signs of a healthy budgie:

Good Appetite: A healthy budgie has a good appetite and will eat regularly. Most budgies eat in the morning and again in the evening. Loss of appetite often indicates that a budgie is sick, injured, or has not yet adapted to an unfamiliar environment.

DID YOU KNOW?
Oldest Budgie

According to the Guinness World Records, the oldest budgie in captivity lived 29 years and 60 days. This long-lived bird was named Charlie and resided in London, England, with his owner, J. Disney. Charlie was born in April 1948 and died on June 20, 1977. The average life span for a budgie in captivity is 15 to 17 years.

Stable Weight: An adult budgie that receives regular exercise and proper nutrition will maintain a fairly stable weight. Budgies often lose their appetite when they are sick, stressed, or depressed, and this can sometimes result in rapid weight loss. During a budgie's natural molting cycle, it is normal for the body weight to temporarily decrease.

Natural Posture: Budgies normally maintain an upright, alert posture. Lying on the bottom of the cage may indicate that a budgie is sick, injured, or frightened.

Activity and Social Interaction: Budgies spend much of their time playing with toys and investigating their surroundings. They also enjoy interacting with their owners and other budgies. Although it is normal for a budgie's activity levels to vary throughout the day, a sudden decrease in activity and social interaction may indicate that a budgie is sick, injured, or depressed.

Vocalization: Healthy budgies are chatty birds. They usually spend many hours each day talking, singing, and chirping to the people, other budgies, and toys in their surroundings. A budgie that isn't vocalizing as much as he normally does could be sick, injured, or frightened.

Regular Breathing: Breathing should be smooth and quiet. If your budgie is sneezing, wheezing, panting with an open beak, or bobbing his tail as he breathes, he could be overheated or have respiratory issues. Temporary panting after strenuous exercise is usually normal.

Photo Courtesy of Diana Cook

Competent Flight: A budgie's normal flight behavior is smooth and steady. A budgie in good health should be able to take off easily, glide smoothly, and land gracefully. Regular flight time outside the cage can help maintain your budgie's flight muscles. A budgie who begins to display difficulty with flying could be ill or injured. Wing clipping and the natural molting cycle can also affect a budgie's ability to fly until new feathers have replaced the old ones.

Clear Eyes: Your budgie's eyes should be clear, bright, and alert. You should not see any redness, discharge, or swelling, which could indicate irritation, an allergic reaction, or a possible infection.

Waxy Cere: The cere (the fleshy area just above the beak) should be smooth and have a waxy appearance. It should not be crusty or peeling. As young budgies approach sexual maturity, it is normal for the cere color to change. Male budgies usually develop a blue cere, and female budgies usually develop a tan or brown cere. During breeding season, mature female budgies often develop a dark brown cere with a flaky texture on the surface, but this is a normal response to hormonal changes. Dirty feathers above the cere is a sign respiratory infection.

Clean Nostrils: The bird's nostrils should be clean and dry. A watery discharge from the nostrils may indicate that your budgie has a respiratory tract infection.

Firm Beak: Your bird's beak should be smooth, firm, and symmetrical, with no cracks. The upper beak should align with the lower beak. Because budgies need a healthy beak to feed and groom themselves, it is important to address beak problems quickly. Consult an avian veterinarian if your budgie's beak appears to be overgrown, rough-textured, or cracked.

Clear Skin: A budgie's skin should be smooth and clear. Red, swollen, or inflamed skin may indicate an infection or an irritation caused by mites.

Bright Plumage: Healthy budgies spend time each day preening, so their feathers should be smooth, silky, and well-groomed. Fluffed-up feathers, damaged feathers, or bald spots may indicate a health problem or feather plucking due to stress.

Smooth Feet: The budgie's feet should be relatively smooth, and his claws should not be too long. Seek the assistance of an avian veterinarian if your budgie's feet show signs of swelling, encrustation, or scabs, as these may be symptoms of a bacterial infection called bumblefoot.

Clean Vent: The cloaca, or vent, and the surrounding feathers should be clean and dry. A watery vent and dirty feathers may indicate digestive problems, parasites, an infection, or a gastrointestinal obstruction. Eating too much watery fruit may also cause a temporary bout of diarrhea, which will usually clear up after the budgie's diet is adjusted.

Healthy Droppings: Your budgie's droppings should be relatively firm and harden rather quickly. The droppings are usually green, with white urates and transparent liquid. The color may change depending on the food you provide for your budgie. Watery droppings are a sign of diarrhea, which usually results from a change in diet, such as from eating too much watery fruit. However, intestinal infections can also cause severe diarrhea.

INFO BOX

The First Molt

Diana Wilkewitz,
Budgiedin Budgerigars

The first molt can begin anywhere from two to six months of age, but most commonly it starts around three months old and can drag on for two to three months.

Before the molt, most baby budgies will have forehead stripes that reach all the way to the cere. They will have dark black eyes with no iris rings. (Or red eyes if it's a red-eyed mutation, still without iris rings.) Some opaline and recessive pied birds will be missing some of their forehead bars, so you won't be able to tell their age based on that. But in general, if you want a baby as young as possible, make sure it has no iris rings and make sure its forehead stripes go all the way to the cere without any bare blotches or pin feathers.

During the first molt, the baby feathers with the forehead stripes will be replaced with feathers that are either all white or all yellow. This will happen unevenly, and the first sign will be a random pin feather here or there. People who have never seen a pin feather before often think there is something stuck to the bird or believe there is something wrong with it. If you can recognize a pin feather, then you will be able to tell that the fewer the bird has, the closer it is to the beginning of its molt, and the more pin feathers and more patches of plain white or yellow feathers, the longer the bird has been molting.

Potential health risks

Common diseases

Although budgies are generally hardy birds, they can contract a number of bacterial and viral illnesses. Being aware of the more common diseases and disorders that can potentially affect these birds can help you take appropriate action before an illness progresses to a more serious stage. Some of the common diseases budgies are susceptible to include:

Avian chlamydiosis (AC): This disease is caused by the bacterium *Chlamydia psittaci*. Although it is sometimes called parrot fever, it attacks many different bird species and is also transmissible to humans. Budgies can catch chlamydiosis through direct exposure to another bird that has the disease or by spending time in an outdoor cage where droppings from infected pigeons or sparrows contaminate the budgie's food or water dish. The disease is often spread between birds and to people through

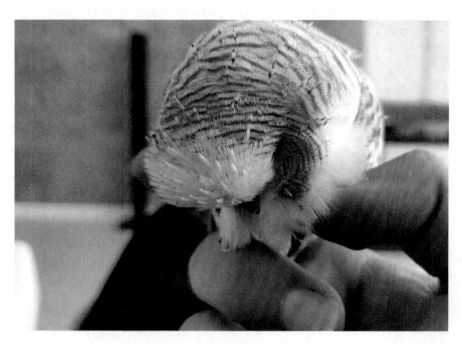

inhaling dust containing dried saliva, mucus, or droppings from infected birds. Direct contact with feathers, droppings, saliva, and contaminated food or water can also transmit the disease.

Symptoms include loss of appetite, lethargy, weight loss, fluffed-up feathers, runny discharge from the eyes or nares, loose green droppings, and breathing difficulties. A veterinarian can perform a combination of tests to diagnose chlamydiosis, and antibiotics are commonly prescribed to treat the disease. In humans, the infection is called psittacosis, and the symptoms are similar to other respiratory illnesses, such as influenza. Antibiotics are commonly prescribed to treat the illness, and most people improve quickly.

CELEBRITY BUDGIES
Churchill's Budgies

Sir Winston Churchill, prime minister of the United Kingdom from 1940 to 1945 and 1951 to 1955, was a proud budgie owner. The distinguished statesman enjoyed training his budgie, Toby, even teaching the bird to carry small salt spoons around the dining room table. Toby enjoyed a place of honor in the prime minister's office and slept in a specially made cage in Churchill's bedroom.

Bumblefoot: Also known as pododermatitis, bumblefoot is a disease that affects the footpads of caged birds. The disease is more common in larger parrots, but budgerigars and cockatiels are also susceptible to the condition. Budgies kept in cages in which all the perches are the same diameter are at increased risk of developing bumblefoot because there is a relatively consistent point of contact between the perches and a particular area of the foot. Perches that are not regularly cleaned are also a potential source of infection.

The infection begins when bacteria enter the body through damaged tissue on the bottom of the feet, leading to redness, swelling, and lameness. As the condition progresses, skin on the footpad may thicken, ulcers may develop, and scabs may form over the affected areas. Regularly examining a budgie's feet can help detect early signs of bumblefoot before the disease progresses. Depending on the severity of the illness, a veterinarian may prescribe antibiotics to fight the bacterial infection and

anti-inflammatory drugs to reduce the swelling.

Avian gastric yeast infection (AGY): Avian gastric yeast infection, or macrorhabdosis, is caused by the yeast *Macrorhabdus ornithogaster*. This highly contagious disease was once called "going light" because it impedes digestion and causes birds to lose weight. The infection is often spread through contaminated drinking water, droppings, and direct contact with infected birds. Once i*nfected, birds may show no outward symptoms until the illness progresses to a more acute stage. As the digestive system becomes inflamed, food is not properly digested, and a budgie will begin to lose weight despite eating normally. Additional* symptoms include lethargy, fluffed-up feathers, repeated vomiting, and undigested seeds in the droppings.

To diagnose an AGY infection, a veterinarian can examine a fecal sample or a smear from the crop or cloaca to detect the presence of *Macrorhabdus ornithogaster. An antifungal medication such as Amphotericin is often effective in treating AGY infections when combined with a special diet to promote recovery.*

Candidiasis: Another fungal infection that can adversely affect the budgerigar's digestive tract is candidiasis, which is caused by a very common environmental yeast called *Candida albicans. Candida* is ordinarily harmless and considered part of the natural microflora population in the avian intestinal tract. However, an imbalance in the normal microflora populations can allow *Candida* to grow out of control and cause a life-threatening infection. This can sometimes happen after a bird has been given a course of antibiotics that unintentionally kills beneficial intestinal bacteria, allowing yeast organisms to multiply and spread. Illnesses that compromise a bird's immune system can also lead to a secondary candidiasis infection, and excessive sugar or carbohydrates in the diet can contribute to the problem. Candidiasis is a common source of crop infection in young budgies called ingluvitis or "sour crop."

Symptoms of candidiasis include loss of appetite, lethargy, fluffed-up feathers, diarrhea, and vomiting. The vomit will have a sour smell, and the crop may swell up as a result of the gasses produced by the yeast. A veterinarian can diagnose candidiasis by examining fluid from the crop or feces to identify the organisms involved. Treatment includes antifungal medications and correcting dietary imbalances to aid the bird in recovery.

Knemidokoptic Mange: Also known as scaly leg and face disease, knemidokoptic mange is a parasitic infection caused by a small, burrowing mite called *Knemidokoptes pilae*. Knemidokoptic mange affects the cere, beak, and feet of several species of pet birds, including budgies, cockatiels, lovebirds, and canaries. The disease is usually transmitted from bird to bird through direct contact. Visible signs of infection include scales and crusts on the cere, beak, legs, and skin around the eyes.

A veterinarian can diagnose the disease by taking a small scraping from the affected area and examining it under a microscope to confirm the presence of *Knemidokoptes* mites. Antiparasitic medications containing ivermectin are often effective in treating the disease.

Avian polyomavirus (APV): Also known as budgerigar fledgling disease, avian polyomavirus is a highly infectious disease that affects a variety of parrot species. Young budgerigars are often severely affected. The virus can be transmitted through contaminated feather dust, droppings, and food fed to young birds by infected adults. The disease typically kills nestling and weanling budgies. Infected birds may stop eating, bleed under the skin, regurgitate food, and develop tremors. Young budgies that survive the initial infection may fail to develop normal primary and secondary wing feathers. Adult birds can carry the virus without symptoms, and infected budgie hens can pass the virus through their eggs. A veterinarian can take a cloacal swab or draw blood to test for the presence of polyomavirus. There is no definitive treatment for the disease.

Health problems

Balanced nutrition plays an essential role in maintaining your budgie's health and promoting longevity. Budgies are vulnerable to a variety of nutrition-related problems, and some of them can be deadly. You can reduce the risk of many common nutritional disorders by ensuring that your budgie receives the essential vitamins and minerals he needs.

Avian Gout: All birds produce uric acid as they metabolize protein. Normally, this waste product is filtered by the kidneys and excreted. Gout occurs when the amount of uric acid in the blood is too high for the kidneys to successfully remove, and uric acid crystals begin to form in the ligaments and joints, or around the liver and kidneys. Symptoms of gout include difficulty walking, swollen joints, weight loss, fluffed-up feathers, and greenish diarrhea. Gout is usually due to kidney damage, which can result from too much salt, protein, or calcium in the diet. Not drinking enough water or drinking water with a high mineral content can also damage the bird's kidneys.

Obesity: Although budgies are small birds, they are prone to obesity when they are fed a high-fat diet and given limited opportunities to exercise. In addition to causing an increased risk of developing arthritis, heart disease, and respiratory problems, obesity can also lead to fatty liver disease (hepatic lipidosis). If you have difficulty feeling your budgie's breastbone, which is located in the middle of the rib cage, your bird may be putting on excess weight. The average budgie weighs between 1.4 oz. and 1.8 oz. A budgie that weighs 2 oz. or more is considered obese. Slowly transitioning your budgie to a balanced diet that includes fruits and vegetables and giving him more opportunities to exercise can help him lose excess weight.

Egg Binding: This serious and sometimes fatal condition occurs when a budgie hen is unable to expel an egg from her body. Symptoms of egg binding include abdominal swelling, fluffed-up feathers, sitting on the cage floor, loss of appetite, and rapid breathing. Take your budgie to a veterinarian if you suspect that she is egg-bound. With prompt treatment, most hens will survive.

Dietary issues are a common cause of egg binding. Insufficient calcium in the diet can cause an egg to develop with a very thin shell or no shell at all, making the egg more prone to becoming stuck. Place a cuttlefish bone or mineral block inside your budgie's cage to provide the dietary calcium she needs to produce healthy eggs.

Feather Plucking: Budgies spend some time each day preening their feathers to keep them in good condition. Feather plucking is an abnormal, self-destructive behavior, and it is a relatively common disorder in pet birds. If you notice your budgie plucking or intentionally damaging his feathers, take your bird to a veterinarian for help in determining the underlying cause. Feather plucking can be triggered by boredom, stress, a skin condition, or other underlying health problems. Nutritional deficiencies can also lead to feather plucking. Birds that do not receive enough calcium or vitamin A in their diet may be more prone to feather plucking. Place a cuttlefish bone or mineral block inside your budgie's cage to help provide necessary calcium and supplement his diet with small portions of fruit and vegetables, including spinach, sweet potato, bell pepper, broccoli, and carrots.

Vitamin A Deficiency: Vitamin A is a very important nutrient for budgies. It is essential for maintaining healthy eyes, skin, bones, and mucus membranes. Because mucus provides a protective layer that helps keep bacteria and other harmful organisms from invading the body, a bird that doesn't receive enough vitamin A is more susceptible to infections. Common symptoms of vitamin A deficiency include dry skin, nasal discharge, sneezing, swollen eyes, respiratory problems, watery droppings, poor feather quality, and feather plucking. Supplementing your budgie's diet with healthy fruits and vegetables can help prevent vitamin A deficiency.

Iodine Deficiency: Budgies are more susceptible to iodine deficiency than many other species of caged birds. A budgie's body needs iodine to produce thyroid hormone, and if there is insufficient iodine in the diet, the thyroid gland may grow larger in order to collect more iodine. The enlargement of the thyroid gland is called goiter or thyroid hyperplasia. The primary symptom of goiter is breathing difficulty, which results

from the enlarged thyroid gland putting pressure on the bird's wind-pipe. A budgie with goiter may also develop a whistle or squeak when it breathes, and other symptoms can include vomiting, lethargy, and difficulty swallowing. If part of your bird's balanced diet includes pelleted bird food formulated for budgies, verify that the pellets you buy are fortified with iodine. As an alternative, place a mineral block that contains iodine and calcium inside your budgie's cage to provide these critical nutrients.

Tumors and cancers

A tumor is a firm mass of tissue or swelling that forms when abnormal cells grow out of control. Tumors may occur on the body, under the skin, or within the body cavity. Although tumors and cancers are not as common in pet birds as they are in dogs and cats, they do occur. Budgies are susceptible to tumors of the adrenal gland, fat cells, kidneys, ovaries, and testes.

Older budgies are more likely to develop a tumor, but they can occur in birds of any age. Tumors may be benign or cancerous, and benign tumors are usually considered less serious than malignant tumors. However, both types can be life-threatening to pet birds due to their small size.

Benign fatty tumors called lipomas commonly occur in budgies that are on a high-fat diet. They usually develop under the skin of the breast-bone or on the abdomen, but they can also occur anywhere on the body. The tumor may be visible as a small lump, or the bird may just seem to be getting fat. When detected early, lipomas can often be successfully reduced by transitioning the bird to a balanced, low-fat diet consisting of pellets, seeds, vegetables, and small portions of fruit. Regular exercise can help a budgie lose excess weight. Surgical removal may be necessary when a tumor has broken through the skin or is making it difficult for a bird to walk or maintain balance.

External tumors are relatively easy to detect. Regularly check your budgie for any unusual lumps or bumps and take your bird to a veterinarian for an examination if you see or feel something abnormal. If a veterinarian determines that a lump is suspicious, a biopsy may be necessary to accurately diagnose the problem. Internal tumors can be more difficult to detect. Some symptoms are the same as those of many other illnesses, including lethargy, loss of appetite, and weight loss. Other symptoms may include an enlarged abdomen, difficulty breathing, or trouble walking or standing.

The best way to determine what is actually causing the problem is to take your budgie to a veterinarian for an examination. Diagnostic tests may include blood tests, X-rays, or an ultrasound. After a tumor has been diagnosed, surgery is often recommended. Other treatment options for cancerous tumors may include chemotherapy, radiation therapy, and synthetic hormone injections to shrink the tumor and prolong life.

Ask the Experts!

Caring for an aging budgie

As budgies age, maintaining their health and happiness requires attentive care. Owners should monitor their bird's diet, adjusting it to prevent obesity and ensuring it is nutrient-rich. Regular vet check-ups are recommended to catch any age-related health issues early. The environment may need to be adapted to accommodate any mobility issues, such as arthritis, by adding flat perches or modifying the cage setup to make it easier for the bird to navigate. Monitoring the bird's behavior and physical condition helps in making necessary adjustments to their care routine.

> *Unless your bird gets unsteady on his feet or flying as he gets older, you should be able to continue the same care. If the bird does need help getting around, you may want to add ladders to the cage so it's easier for him to navigate. You may want to ease up on the wing clipping at that time as well, but it depends on the individual bird. Be aware of how your budgie is getting around and do what you can to make it easier for him."*

ANITA GOLDEN,
formerly Nita's Nest

> *Budgies need to see an avian vet at least once a year for a wellness checkup. Weigh your budgie weekly and keep a weight chart so you can compare weight from one week to the next. Also write down what your budgie is eating and his daily routine (flying around, playing outside the cage, etc.). As your budgie gets older, make sure his feet are good (have different types of perches to avoid bumblefoot) and make sure there are not any drafts around the cage."*

DIANE P HYDE,
Long Island Parrot Society

> " As a budgie gets older, providing flat platform perches and vet wrapping anything super hard can help alleviate pain in joints and feet. Just keep an eye on the condition of the vet wrap and replace as needed. If an older budgie likes to sit on the bottom grate of a cage frequently, providing softer areas to perch there will help as well."

SHANNON COCHRAN,
Chesapeake Aviary

> " Watch for fatty liver problems, which may cause a fatty lipoma. Many times this will cause the beak and nails to overgrow. Observe the bird from a distance and watch to see if it acts normally, chirps normally, and has normal-looking droppings. Look at the bottom of the cage and see what the bird is chewing up, whether it's toys or feather mutilation issues."

PAUL LEWIS,
Birds Unlimited

CHAPTER 9

The Joy of Budgies

Love from your budgie

Affection

People show their affection in many different ways: by sharing physical touch, giving gifts, talking and singing, and spending time with someone special. Humans aren't the only ones with the capacity to express affection. While they may not convey their emotions in exactly

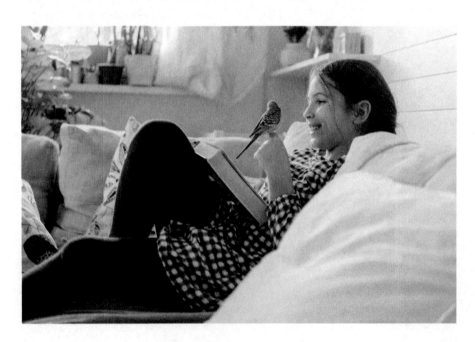

the same way that we do, animals display a variety of behaviors that demonstrate strong emotional bonds with their own kind and with other species. Budgies are naturally affectionate, and they show their affection in a number of ways, but their behavior can be confusing to those who aren't familiar with the sounds and visual signals they use to communicate with other birds and humans.

Budgies are social birds, and one of the primary ways they communicate with their flock members is by sound. Like many animals, budgies often use vocalizations to affirm their affection. Budgies chirp, whistle, warble, and sing when they are happy and relaxed and when they want to interact with other birds or their human caretakers. They sometimes express feelings of contentment by making a soft, crackling sound with their beaks before going to sleep. The noise they generate as they grind their beaks may sound strange to our ears, but it's a clear indication that a budgie feels safe and secure.

Budgies also use their beaks in other ways to strengthen social bonds. Two budgies might gently nibble on each other or tap their beaks together as a sign of affection. If they really like each other, one budgie may regurgitate food and share it with a friend as a gesture of deep respect and companionship. Humans and many animals also use eye contact to express various emotions. Budgies and other parrots use a form of non-verbal communication called "eye pinning" to reveal their current emotional state. When a budgie is pinning his eyes, the pupils rapidly dilate and contract. This usually indicates that a bird is happy, excited, or intensely curious about another bird or animal, a human, or an inanimate object.

Budgies employ a variety of physical movements and gestures in other ways to convey their affection. They may stand in place and flap their wings when they are happy or if they want attention, and they may wag their tail like a dog when they feel joyful. Mutual grooming is another behavior that budgies use to reinforce social bonds. Although it serves a practical purpose by keeping their feathers in good condition, mutual grooming, or allopreening, is also one of the primary ways budgies display affection to prospective mates and close companions.

CELEBRITY BUDGIES
Sparkie Williams

A verbose budgie named Sparkie Williams gained international fame when he starred in an ad campaign for Capern's Bird Seed. Capern's ad campaign featured a voice recording of Sparkie, designed to teach birds to talk, and sold over 20,000 copies. Known as "the most talkative bird of all time," Sparkie lived from 1954 to 1962 and could speak more than 500 words. This remarkable bird also inspired the 1977 opera Pretty Talk by Michael Nyman. After his death on December 4, 1962, Sparkie was taxidermied and displayed in a museum in Newcastle.

Love for owners

Budgies show affection toward people in much the same way they display affection toward each other. Budgies are intelligent birds, and they can recognize the faces and voices of those who care for them. Once your budgie has become comfortable in your presence and has learned to trust you, he will begin to form a strong emotional bond with you. One way budgies display affection for their owners is by whistling and making noise when they enter the room. If you teach your budgie to whistle or to say a few words and phrases, he will likely repeat them whenever you appear to show how happy he is to see you.

Budgies like to have physical contact with the people they trust. When they are let out of the cage to exercise or play, they may perch on your shoulder, climb on you, rub their head against you, and even attempt to groom your hair or clothing. Gently nibbling with their beaks, without trying to bite, is another sign of budgie affection. You can show your appreciation for these displays by gently scratching your bird's head

in return, especially if he bows his head in front of you to signal that he would like to be petted.

If you notice your budgie hanging upside down in his cage, it is another indication that your bird is fond of you. Birds occasionally like to hang upside down, but it puts them in a vulnerable position, and they avoid doing this in the presence of others unless they feel safe. Like people, budgies enjoy spending time with their companions, so try to spend some quality time with your budgie every day to establish a strong and lasting bond.

Love for other budgies

Budgies usually enjoy each other's company, and they display their affection in many different ways. Budgie companions often perch side by side and chatter to each other like two old friends sitting on a park bench. Just as people enjoy sharing a meal together, budgies will often eat together with a close friend. During courtship, a budgie male will take this a step further by feeding regurgitated food to a prospective mate to demonstrate that he is a good provider. Sharing food is not limited to courtship rituals; it is also a common sign of affection between budgie friends.

People like to sing and dance with their friends, and budgies are no different. Budgies sing when they are happy and comfortable in their surroundings, and they will sing, hop around, and bob their heads when they enjoy the company of another bird. This, too, can be part of a courtship display, but male budgies also enjoy singing and dancing for male friends or just to show off. Budgies groom and preen their feathers several times a day, and they use these grooming sessions to strengthen emotional bonds with mates and close friends, regardless of gender.

Budgie buddies delight in grooming each other, paying particular attention to the areas on the head and face that an individual bird cannot reach by himself. Budgies have individual personalities, however, and sometimes two birds may simply not get along, even if they have been gradually introduced to each other to avoid territorial conflicts.

If two birds squawk at each other, peck or bite in an unfriendly way, or begin to fight, you will need to put them in separate cages. You can try to gradually introduce them another time and monitor their behavior to determine whether they can be together in the same cage or should remain apart.

Photo Courtesy of
Diana Cook

Cuddling and kissing

When budgies like each other, they will often sit on a perch together and cuddle up close. While budgies enjoy physical contact with other budgies and with people, they are delicate birds and must be handled carefully. They also have distinct personalities, and some budgies prefer not to be handled. Picking them up to hold or cuddle them may frighten them. But even though some budgies don't like being handled, they may still enjoy some types of physical contact on their own terms. They may fly onto your shoulder and snuggle up against your neck or perch on your finger to show their affection. Budgies also appear to "kiss" each other by tapping their beaks together or interlocking their beaks to share food.

Budgies sometimes attempt to kiss people the same way. If you want to kiss your budgie, give him a gentle kiss on the top of the head rather than kissing him on the beak. Kissing your bird on the beak can transfer human saliva that contains thousands of different bacteria that birds don't have, and their immune systems are not able to protect them. There is also a chance that your budgie could transfer an infection to you. Psittacosis is a disease that birds in the parrot family can get, and the disease can be spread to humans. The symptoms can range from very mild to very serious.

Fun facts about budgies

Fun facts

- Although all budgies are parakeets, not all parakeets are budgies. There are about 115 different species of parakeets around the world, and they come in a variety of shapes, sizes and colors.
- Budgies have between 2,000 and 3,000 feathers.
- There are two different types of budgies: the traditional budgie that you commonly see in pet stores and the larger English budgie, which was bred for shows and exhibitions. The traditional budgie is

around 7 to 9 inches tall, while the English budgie is usually around 10 to 12 inches tall.

- Budgies are one of the most popular pets in the world, ranking just below dogs and cats.
- You can often tell a male budgie from a female budgie by the color of the fleshy area just above the beak, which is called the cere. A male budgie usually has a blue cere, and a female budgie usually has a white, pink, or brown cere.
- Budgerigar is the more formal name for a budgie. The name comes from "betcherrygah," an Australian Aboriginal language name for these birds.
- A budgie named Charlie lived for over 29 years, longer than any other budgie.
- Most birds have three toes that point forward and one toe that points backward. Budgies and other parrots have two toes that point forward and two toes that point backward.

- Budgie eggs are covered with tiny holes that let oxygen into the shell and let carbon dioxide out. This allows budgie chicks to breathe while they are growing inside the eggshell.

- Although people are used to seeing budgies in a wide variety of colors in pet shops, the natural color of wild budgies in Australia is bright yellow and green, with black markings on the wings.

- Budgies can turn their head 180 degrees to look in all directions. You can see budgies turn their head and cover it with their wing when they prepare to go to sleep.

- The heart rate of a healthy budgie will range from about 275 beats per minute when resting, to about 600 beats per minute when flying or exercising.

- Budgies can learn to talk better than some larger parrots. A budgie named Puck holds the record for having the largest vocabulary of any bird. He could say 1,728 words!

- Budgies make a scratchy sound with their beaks when they are contented and relaxed. This behavior is called "beak grinding," and it helps them keep their beaks trim and in proper shape.

Conclusion

What is it about budgies that continues to capture the hearts of pet owners all over the world? Is it because they are small and easy to care for? Or because they are highly intelligent and easy to train? Or is it because they are sociable and affectionate, and thrive on spending time with their owners? Certainly, all of these attributes contribute to the budgie's ongoing popularity, but perhaps there are other reasons that are more difficult to define. Recent studies have shown that seeing and hearing birds is associated with improved mental health and that interacting with birds tends to have a calming effect on people. Little wonder that people have been keeping various parrot species as pets for thousands of years.

Because budgies are playful and form strong attachments with their owners, they make great pets for families with children who are old enough to understand how to handle them gently. Unlike larger pets that require more space for exercise, budgies can get plenty of exercise in a small room, so they are a perfect fit for small houses or apartments. Budgies come in a variety of beautiful colors, and just having them around will brighten any room. Because they are small birds, budgies have modest appetites and their diet is based on seed, so feeding them is relatively inexpensive. By providing your budgie with a balanced diet of pellets, seed, small portions of fruit and vegetables, and a mineral block for essential nutrients, you will keep him happy and healthy for many years to come. Although caring for a budgie is a responsibility, it is also a wonderful experience that will bring great joy to your life.

Printed in Great Britain
by Amazon

56513528R00079